Recorder
Scales, Arpeggios & Exercises

for Trinity College London
Descant & Treble Recorder
exams from 2017

Initial-Grade 8

Published by
Trinity College London Press
www.trinitycollege.com

Registered in England
Company no. 09726123

Descant Recorder
Initial

Candidate to prepare *either* section i) *or* section ii) in full					
either **i) Scales & triads** (from memory) – the examiner will select from the following:					
Scales: G and D major (first five notes only)	ascending and descending	min. ♩ = 60	tongued		*mf*
Triads: G and D major		min. ♪ = 120			
or **ii) Exercises** (music may be used):					
Candidate to prepare 1a *or* 1b; 2a *or* 2b; and 3a *or* 3b (three exercises in total). The candidate will choose one exercise to play first; the examiner will then select one of the remaining two prepared exercises to be performed.					
1a. Steady Now	*or*	1b. Top to Bottom	for tone and phrasing		
2a. Spider in the Sink!	*or*	2b. Upstairs	for articulation		
3a. In Threes	*or*	3b. Round and Round	for finger technique		

i) Scales & triads

G major scale (first five notes only)

G major triad

D major scale (first five notes only)

D major triad

ii) Exercises

1a. Steady Now – tone and phrasing

1b. Top to Bottom – tone and phrasing

2a. Spider in the Sink! – articulation

2b. Upstairs – articulation

3a. In Threes – finger technique

3b. Round and Round – finger technique

Descant Recorder
Grade 1

Candidate to prepare *either* section i) *or* section ii) in full				
either **i) Scales & arpeggios** (from memory) – the examiner will select from the following:				
Scales: F and C major D minor (candidate's choice of *either* harmonic *or* melodic *or* natural minor) **Arpeggios:** F and C major D minor	one octave	min. tempi: scales: ♩ = 72 arpeggios: ♪ = 120	tongued *or* slurred	*mf*
or **ii) Exercises** (music may be used):				
Candidate to prepare 1a *or* 1b; 2a *or* 2b; and 3a *or* 3b (three exercises in total). The candidate will choose one exercise to play first; the examiner will then select one of the remaining two prepared exercises to be performed.				
1a. Go East *or* 1b. Kyoto			for tone and phrasing	
2a. Log Drum *or* 2b. Marcial			for articulation	
3a. Arpeggioni *or* 3b. The Third Way			for finger technique	

i) Scales & arpeggios

F major scale (one octave)

F major arpeggio (one octave)

C major scale (one octave)

C major arpeggio (one octave)

D harmonic minor scale (one octave)

D melodic minor scale (one octave)

D natural minor scale (one octave)

D minor arpeggio (one octave)

ii) Exercises

1a. Go East – tone and phrasing

1b. Kyoto – tone and phrasing

Descant Recorder Grade 1 continued

2a. Log Drum – articulation

2b. Marcial – articulation

3a. Arpeggioni – finger technique

3b. The Third Way – finger technique

Treble Recorder
Grade 1

Candidate to prepare *either* section i) *or* section ii) in full					
either i) Scales & arpeggios (from memory) − the examiner will select from the following:					
Scales: Bb and F major G minor (candidate's choice of *either* harmonic *or* melodic *or* natural minor)	one octave	min. tempi: scales: ♩ = 72 arpeggios: ♪ = 120	tongued *or* slurred	*mf*	
Arpeggios: Bb and F major G minor					
or ii) Exercises (music may be used):					
Candidate to prepare 1a *or* 1b; 2a *or* 2b; and 3a *or* 3b (three exercises in total). The candidate will choose one exercise to play first; the examiner will then select one of the remaining two prepared exercises to be performed.					
1a. Go East	*or*	1b. Kyoto	for tone and phrasing		
2a. Log Drum	*or*	2b. Marcial	for articulation		
3a. Arpeggioni	*or*	3b. The Third Way	for finger technique		

i) Scales & arpeggios

Bb major scale (one octave)

Bb major arpeggio (one octave)

F major scale (one octave) − see Descant Recorder Grade 1 page 4

F major arpeggio (one octave) − see Descant Recorder Grade 1 page 4

G harmonic minor scale (one octave)

G melodic minor scale (one octave)

Treble Recorder Grade 1 continued

G natural minor scale (one octave)

G minor arpeggio (one octave)

ii) Exercises

1a. Go East – tone and phrasing

1b. Kyoto – tone and phrasing

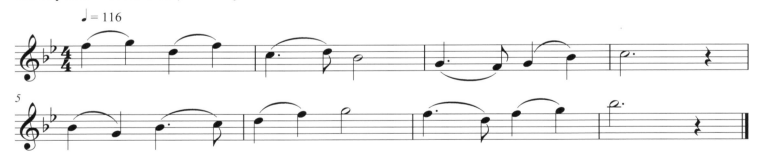

2a. Log Drum – articulation

2b. Marcial – articulation

3a. Arpeggioni – finger technique

3b. The Third Way – finger technique

Descant Recorder
Grade 2

Candidate to prepare *either* section i) *or* section ii) in full				
either i) **Scales & arpeggios** (from memory) – the examiner will select from the following:				
Scales: D major D minor (candidate's choice of *either* harmonic *or* melodic *or* natural minor)	to 12th	min. tempi: scales: ♩ = 72 arpeggios: ♪ = 120	tongued *or* slurred	*mf*
G major	one octave and down to the dominant			
E minor (candidate's choice of *either* harmonic *or* melodic *or* natural minor)	one octave			
Arpeggios: D major D minor	to 12th			
G major	one octave and down to the dominant			
E minor	one octave			
or ii) **Exercises** (music may be used):				
Candidate to prepare 1a *or* 1b; 2a *or* 2b; and 3a *or* 3b (three exercises in total). The candidate will choose one exercise to play first; the examiner will then select one of the remaining two prepared exercises to be performed.				
1a. Minor Steps	*or*	1b. Shaping	for tone and phrasing	
2a. Echo Swing	*or*	2b. Some Cuckoo	for articulation	
3a. Jazz Hands	*or*	3b. Off and On	for finger technique	

i) Scales & arpeggios

D major scale (to 12th)

D major arpeggio (to 12th)

D harmonic minor scale (to 12th)

D melodic minor scale (to 12th)

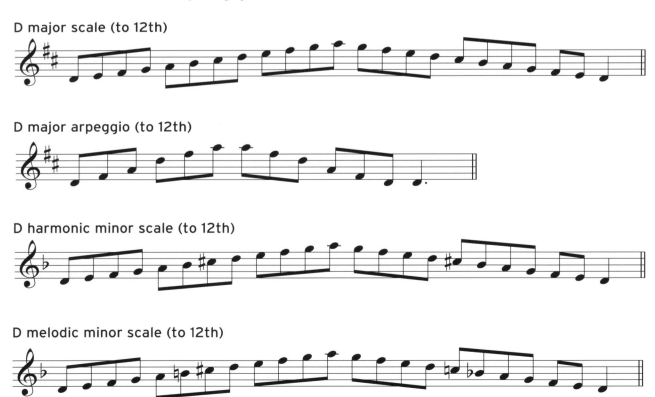

D natural minor scale (to 12th)

D minor arpeggio (to 12th)

G major scale (one octave and down to the dominant)

G major arpeggio (one octave and down to the dominant)

E harmonic minor scale (one octave)

E melodic minor scale (one octave)

E natural minor scale (one octave)

E minor arpeggio (one octave)

ii) Exercises

1a. Minor Steps – tone and phrasing

1b. Shaping – tone and phrasing

2a. Echo Swing – articulation

2b. Some Cuckoo – articulation

3a. Jazz Hands – finger technique

3b. Off and On – finger technique

Treble Recorder
Grade 2

Candidate to prepare *either* section i) *or* section ii) in full					
either i) **Scales & arpeggios** (from memory) − the examiner will select from the following:					
Scales: G major G minor (candidate's choice of *either* harmonic *or* melodic *or* natural minor)		to 12th	min. tempi: scales: ♩ = 72 arpeggios: ♪ = 120	tongued *or* slurred	*mf*
C major		one octave and down to the dominant			
A minor (candidate's choice of *either* harmonic *or* melodic *or* natural minor)		one octave			
Arpeggios: G major G minor		to 12th			
C major		one octave and down to the dominant			
A minor		one octave			
or ii) **Exercises** (music may be used):					
Candidate to prepare 1a *or* 1b; 2a *or* 2b; and 3a *or* 3b (three exercises in total). The candidate will choose one exercise to play first; the examiner will then select one of the remaining two prepared exercises to be performed.					
1a. Minor Steps	*or*	1b. Shaping	for tone and phrasing		
2a. Echo Swing	*or*	2b. Some Cuckoo	for articulation		
3a. Jazz Hands	*or*	3b. Off and On	for finger technique		

i) Scales & arpeggios

G major scale (to 12th)

G major arpeggio (to 12th)

G harmonic minor scale (to 12th)

G melodic minor scale (to 12th)

G natural minor scale (to 12th)

G minor arpeggio (to 12th)

C major scale (one octave and down to the dominant)

C major arpeggio (one octave and down to the dominant)

A harmonic minor scale (one octave)

A melodic minor scale (one octave)

A natural minor scale (one octave)

A minor arpeggio (one octave)

ii) Exercises

1a. Minor Steps – tone and phrasing

legato e espressivo

1b. Shaping – tone and phrasing

2a. Echo Swing – articulation

2b. Some Cuckoo – articulation

♩ = 108

3a. Jazz Hands – finger technique

Swing ♩ = 132

3b. Off and On – finger technique

♩ = 138

Descant Recorder
Grade 3

Candidate to prepare *either* section i) *or* section ii) in full					
either i) **Scales & arpeggios** (from memory) − the examiner will select from the following:					
Scales: E minor (candidate's choice of *either* harmonic *or* melodic minor)	to 12th	min. tempi: scales: ♩ = 84 arpeggios: ♪ = 132	tongued *or* slurred	*mf*
F and B♭ major	one octave and down to the dominant			
A and G minor (candidate's choice of *either* harmonic *or* melodic minor)	one octave			
Chromatic scale starting on G				
Arpeggios: E minor	to 12th			
F and B♭ major	one octave and down to the dominant			
A and G minor	one octave			
or ii) **Exercises** (music may be used):					
Candidate to prepare 1a *or* 1b; 2a *or* 2b; and 3a *or* 3b (three exercises in total).					
The candidate will choose one exercise to play first; the examiner will then select one of the remaining two prepared exercises to be performed.					
1a. A Major Event	*or*	1b. Espressivo	for tone and phrasing		
2a. On Tiptoe	*or*	2b. Ornamental Garden	for articulation		
3a. A Smoothie	*or*	3b. Wedding Dance	for finger technique		

i) Scales & arpeggios

E harmonic minor scale (to 12th)

E melodic minor scale (to 12th)

E minor arpeggio (to 12th)

F major scale (one octave and down to the dominant)

F major arpeggio (one octave and down to the dominant)

Bb major scale (one octave and down to the dominant)

Bb major arpeggio (one octave and down to the dominant)

A harmonic minor scale (one octave) – see Treble Recorder Grade 2 page 15

A melodic minor scale (one octave) – see Treble Recorder Grade 2 page 15

A minor arpeggio (one octave) – see Treble Recorder Grade 2 page 15

G harmonic minor scale (one octave) – see Treble Recorder Grade 1 page 7

G melodic minor scale (one octave) – see Treble Recorder Grade 1 page 7

G minor arpeggio (one octave) – see Treble Recorder Grade 1 page 8

Chromatic scale starting on G (one octave)

ii) Exercises

1a. A Major Event – tone and phrasing

1b. Espressivo – tone and phrasing

2a. On Tiptoe – articulation

2b. Ornamental Garden – articulation

3a. A Smoothie – finger technique

3b. Wedding Dance – finger technique

Treble Recorder
Grade 3

Candidate to prepare *either* section i) *or* section ii) in full					
either **i) Scales & arpeggios** (from memory) – the examiner will select from the following:					
Scales: A minor (candidate's choice of *either* harmonic *or* melodic minor)	to 12th		min. tempi: scales: ♩ = 84 arpeggios: ♪ = 132	tongued *or* slurred	*mf*
Bb and Eb major	one octave and down to the dominant				
D and C minor (candidate's choice of *either* harmonic *or* melodic minor)	one octave				
Chromatic scale starting on C					
Arpeggios: A minor	to 12th				
Bb and Eb major	one octave and down to the dominant				
D and C minor	one octave				
or **ii) Exercises** (music may be used):					
Candidate to prepare 1a *or* 1b; 2a *or* 2b; and 3a *or* 3b (three exercises in total).					
The candidate will choose one exercise to play first; the examiner will then select one of the remaining two prepared exercises to be performed.					
1a. A Major Event	*or*	1b. Espressivo	for tone and phrasing		
2a. On Tiptoe	*or*	2b. Ornamental Garden	for articulation		
3a. A Smoothie	*or*	3b. Wedding Dance	for finger technique		

i) Scales & arpeggios

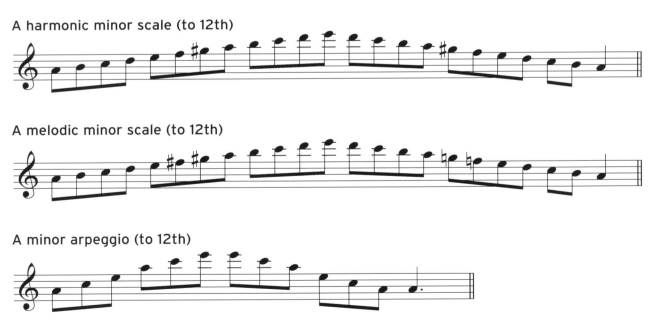

A harmonic minor scale (to 12th)

A melodic minor scale (to 12th)

A minor arpeggio (to 12th)

Bb major scale (one octave and down to the dominant) – see Descant Recorder Grade 3 page 19

Bb major arpeggio (one octave and down to the dominant) – see Descant Recorder Grade 3 page 19

Eb major scale (one octave and down to the dominant)

Eb major arpeggio (one octave and down to the dominant)

D harmonic minor scale (one octave)

D melodic minor scale (one octave)

D minor arpeggio (one octave)

C harmonic minor scale (one octave)

C melodic minor scale (one octave)

C minor arpeggio (one octave)

Chromatic scale starting on C (one octave)

ii) Exercises

1a. A Major Event – tone and phrasing

1b. Espressivo – tone and phrasing

2a. On Tiptoe – articulation

2b. Ornamental Garden – articulation

3a. A Smoothie – finger technique

3b. Wedding Dance – finger technique

Descant Recorder
Grade 4

Candidate to prepare *either* section i) *or* section ii) in full				
either i) **Scales & arpeggios** (from memory) – the examiner will select from the following:				
Scales: C major	two octaves			
E♭ major	to 12th	min. tempi: scales: ♩ = 96 arpeggios: ♪ = 138 7ths: ♩ = 69	tongued *or* slurred	*mf*
A major A and B minor (candidate's choice of *either* harmonic *or* melodic minor)	one octave and down to the dominant			
F♯ minor (candidate's choice of *either* harmonic *or* melodic minor)	one octave			
Chromatic scale starting on C (tongued only)	two octaves			
Pentatonic (major) scale starting on F	one octave			
Arpeggios: C major	two octaves			
E♭ major	to 12th			
A major A and B minor	one octave and down to the dominant			
F♯ minor	one octave			
Dominant 7th in the key of F	two octaves			
or ii) **Exercises** (music may be used):				
Candidate to prepare 1a *or* 1b; 2a *or* 2b; and 3a *or* 3b (three exercises in total).				
The candidate will choose one exercise to play first; the examiner will then select one of the remaining two prepared exercises to be performed.				
1a. Balancing Act	*or*	1b. Converse	for tone and phrasing	
2a. Dainty	*or*	2b. Nice Groove	for articulation	
3a. Cheeky	*or*	3b. Sharpish	for finger technique	

i) Scales & arpeggios

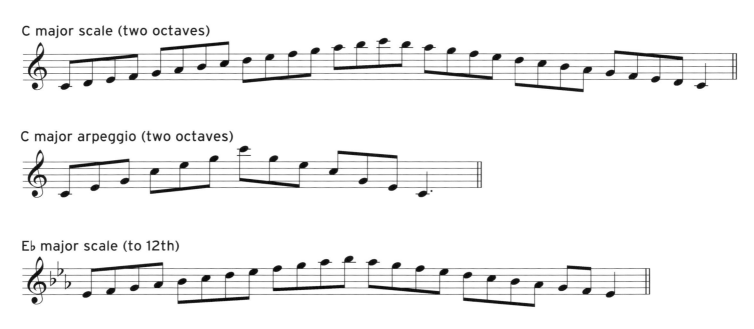

C major scale (two octaves)

C major arpeggio (two octaves)

E♭ major scale (to 12th)

Eb major arpeggio (to 12th)

A major scale (one octave and down to the dominant)

A major arpeggio (one octave and down to the dominant)

A harmonic minor scale (one octave and down to the dominant)

A melodic minor scale (one octave and down to the dominant)

A minor arpeggio (one octave and down to the dominant)

B harmonic minor scale (one octave and down to the dominant)

B melodic minor scale (one octave and down to the dominant)

Descant Recorder Grade 4 continued

B minor arpeggio (one octave and down to the dominant)

F# harmonic minor scale (one octave)

F# melodic minor scale (one octave)

F# minor arpeggio (one octave)

Chromatic scale starting on C – tongued only (two octaves)

Pentatonic (major) scale starting on F (one octave)

Dominant 7th in the key of F (two octaves)

ii) Exercises

1a. Balancing Act – tone and phrasing

1b. Converse – tone and phrasing

2a. Dainty – articulation

Descant Recorder Grade 4 continued

2b. Nice Groove – articulation

3a. Cheeky – finger technique

3b. Sharpish – finger technique

Treble Recorder
Grade 4

Candidate to prepare *either* section i) *or* section ii) in full				
either i) Scales & arpeggios (from memory) − the examiner will select from the following:				
Scales: F major	two octaves	min. tempi: scales: ♩ = 96 arpeggios: ♪ = 138 7ths: ♩ = 69	tongued *or* slurred	*mf*
A♭ major	to 12th			
D major D and E minor (candidate's choice of *either* harmonic *or* melodic minor)	one octave and down to the dominant			
B minor (candidate's choice of *either* harmonic *or* melodic minor)	one octave			
Chromatic scale starting on F (tongued only)	two octaves			
Pentatonic (major) scale starting on B♭	one octave			
Arpeggios: F major	two octaves			
A♭ major	to 12th			
D major D and E minor	one octave and down to the dominant			
B minor	one octave			
Dominant 7th in the key of B♭	two octaves			
or ii) Exercises (music may be used):				
Candidate to prepare 1a *or* 1b; 2a *or* 2b; and 3a *or* 3b (three exercises in total). The candidate will choose one exercise to play first; the examiner will then select one of the remaining two prepared exercises to be performed.				
1a. Balancing Act	*or*	1b. Converse	for tone and phrasing	
2a. Dainty	*or*	2b. Nice Groove	for articulation	
3a. Cheeky	*or*	3b. Sharpish	for finger technique	

i) Scales & arpeggios

F major scale (two octaves)

F major arpeggio (two octaves)

A♭ major scale (to 12th)

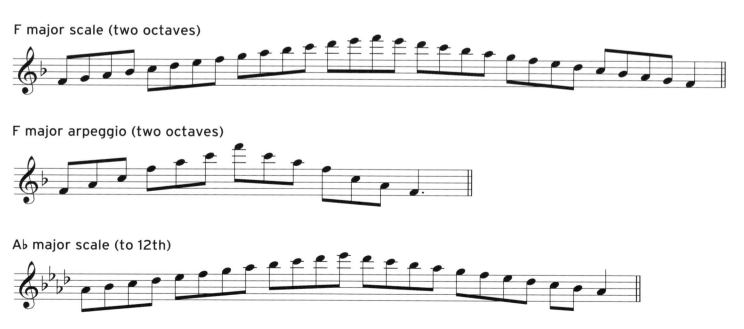

Treble Recorder Grade 4 continued

Ab major arpeggio (to 12th)

D major scale (one octave and down to the dominant)

D major arpeggio (one octave and down to the dominant)

D harmonic minor scale (one octave and down to the dominant)

D melodic minor scale (one octave and down to the dominant)

D minor arpeggio (one octave and down to the dominant)

E harmonic minor scale (one octave and down to the dominant)

E melodic minor scale (one octave and down to the dominant)

E minor arpeggio (one octave and down to the dominant)

B harmonic minor scale (one octave)

B melodic minor scale (one octave)

B minor arpeggio (one octave)

Chromatic scale starting on F – tongued only (two octaves)

Pentatonic (major) scale starting on B♭ (one octave)

Dominant 7th in the key of B♭ (two octaves)

ii) Exercises

1a. **Balancing Act** – tone and phrasing

1b. **Converse** – tone and phrasing

2a. **Dainty** – articulation

2b. Nice Groove – articulation

3a. Cheeky – finger technique

3b. Sharpish – finger technique

Descant Recorder
Grade 5

Candidate to prepare *either* section i) *or* section ii) in full				
either **i) Scales & arpeggios** (from memory) − the examiner will select from the following:				
Scales: C minor (candidate's choice of *either* harmonic *or* melodic minor)	two octaves			
E, Eb and G major F and C# minor (candidate's choice of *either* harmonic *or* melodic minor)	to 12th			
Ab major F# minor (candidate's choice of *either* harmonic *or* melodic minor)	one octave and down to the dominant	min. tempi: scales: ♩ = 116 arpeggios: ♪ = 152 7ths: ♩ = 76	tongued *or* slurred	*mf*
Chromatic scale starting on C Pentatonic (major) scale starting on C	two octaves			
Arpeggios: C minor				
E, Eb and G major F and C# minor	to 12th			
Ab major F# minor	one octave and down to the dominant			
Diminished 7th starting on C	two octaves			
Dominant 7ths in the keys of A and Db	one octave			
or **ii) Exercises** (music may be used):				
Candidate to prepare 1a *or* 1b; 2a *or* 2b; and 3a *or* 3b (three exercises in total). The candidate will choose one exercise to play first; the examiner will then select one of the remaining two prepared exercises to be performed.				
1a. Persuasion *or* 1b. Sequences	for tone and phrasing			
2a. Good Effects *or* 2b. Left, Right!	for articulation			
3a. Minor Debate *or* 3b. Trills and Spills	for finger technique			

i) Scales & arpeggios

C harmonic minor scale (two octaves)

C melodic minor scale (two octaves)

C minor arpeggio (two octaves)

E major scale (to 12th)

E major arpeggio (to 12th)

Eb major scale (to 12th) − see Descant Recorder Grade 4 page 26

Eb major arpeggio (to 12th) − see Descant Recorder Grade 4 page 27

G major scale (to 12th) − see Treble Recorder Grade 2 page 14

G major arpeggio (to 12th) − see Treble Recorder Grade 2 page 14

F harmonic minor scale (to 12th)

F melodic minor scale (to 12th)

F minor arpeggio (to 12th)

C# harmonic minor scale (to 12th)

Descant Recorder Grade 5 continued

C# melodic minor scale (to 12th)

C# minor arpeggio (to 12th)

Ab major scale (one octave and down to the dominant)

Ab major arpeggio (one octave and down to the dominant)

F# harmonic minor scale (one octave and down to the dominant)

F# melodic minor scale (one octave and down to the dominant)

F# minor arpeggio (one octave and down to the dominant)

Chromatic scale starting on C (two octaves)

Pentatonic (major) scale starting on C (two octaves)

Diminished 7th starting on C (two octaves)

Dominant 7th in the key of A (one octave)

Dominant 7th in the key of D♭ (one octave)

ii) Exercises

1a. Persuasion – tone and phrasing

Descant Recorder Grade 5 continued

1b. Sequences – tone and phrasing

2a. Good Effects – articulation

* flutter tongue or finger vibrato

2b. Left, Right! – articulation

3a. Minor Debate – finger technique

3b. Trills and Spills – finger technique

Treble Recorder
Grade 5

Candidate to prepare *either* section i) *or* section ii) in full				
either **i) Scales & arpeggios** (from memory) − the examiner will select from the following:				
Scales: F minor (candidate's choice of *either* harmonic *or* melodic minor)	two octaves		min. tempi: scales: ♩ = 116 arpeggios: ♪ = 152 7ths: ♩ = 76	tongued *or* slurred	*mf*
A, A♭ and C major B♭ and F♯ minor (candidate's choice of *either* harmonic *or* melodic minor)	to 12th				
D♭ major B minor (candidate's choice of *either* harmonic *or* melodic minor)	one octave and down to the dominant				
Chromatic scale starting on F Pentatonic (major) scale starting on F	two octaves				
Arpeggios: F minor					
A, A♭ and C major B♭ and F♯ minor	to 12th				
D♭ major B minor	one octave and down to the dominant				
Diminished 7th starting on F	two octaves				
Dominant 7ths in the keys of D and G♭	one octave				
or **ii) Exercises** (music may be used):				
Candidate to prepare 1a *or* 1b; 2a *or* 2b; and 3a *or* 3b (three exercises in total).				
The candidate will choose one exercise to play first; the examiner will then select one of the remaining two prepared exercises to be performed.				
1a. Persuasion	*or*	1b. Sequences	for tone and phrasing	
2a. Good Effects	*or*	2b. Left, Right!	for articulation	
3a. Minor Debate	*or*	3b. Trills and Spills	for finger technique	

i) Scales & arpeggios

F harmonic minor scale (two octaves)

F melodic minor scale (two octaves)

F minor arpeggio (two octaves)

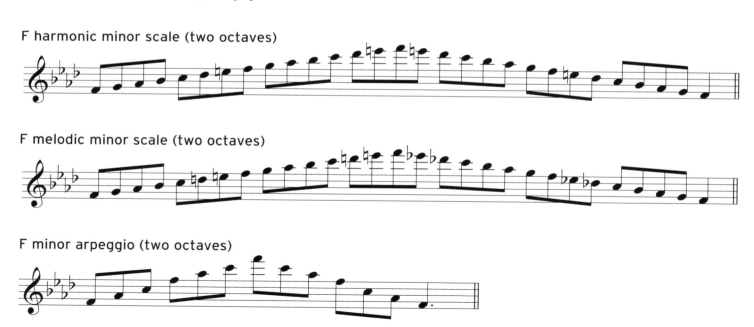

A major scale (to 12th)

A major arpeggio (to 12th)

Ab major scale (to 12th) – see Treble Recorder Grade 4 page 31

Ab major arpeggio (to 12th) – see Treble Recorder Grade 4 page 32

C major scale (to 12th)

C major arpeggio (to 12th)

Bb harmonic minor scale (to 12th)

Bb melodic minor scale (to 12th)

Bb minor arpeggio (to 12th)

Treble Recorder Grade 5 continued

F# harmonic minor scale (to 12th)

F# melodic minor scale (to 12th)

F# minor arpeggio (to 12th)

Db major scale (one octave and down to the dominant)

Db major arpeggio (one octave and down to the dominant)

B harmonic minor scale (one octave and down to the dominant) – see Descant Recorder Grade 4 page 27

B melodic minor scale (one octave and down to the dominant) – see Descant Recorder Grade 4 page 27

B minor arpeggio (one octave and down to the dominant) – see Descant Recorder Grade 4 page 28

Chromatic scale starting on F (two octaves)

Pentatonic (major) scale starting on F (two octaves)

Diminished 7th starting on F (two octaves)

Dominant 7th in the key of D (one octave)

Dominant 7th in the key of G♭ (one octave)

ii) Exercises

1a. Persuasion – tone and phrasing

Treble Recorder Grade 5 continued

1b. Sequences – tone and phrasing

2a. Good Effects – articulation

* flutter tongue or finger vibrato

2b. Left, Right! – articulation

3a. Minor Debate – finger technique

3b. Trills and Spills – finger technique

Treble Recorder
Grade 6

Candidate to prepare *either* section i) *or* section ii) in full				
either i) **Scales & arpeggios** (from memory) – the examiner will select from the following:				
Candidates should prepare scales and arpeggios from the following tonal centres: F major, F minor	two octaves	min. tempi: scales: ♩ = 120 arpeggios: ♩. = 63 7ths: ♩ = 96	tongued, slurred *or* staccato- tongued	*mf*
A major, A minor	to 12th			
E♭ major, E♭ minor	one octave and down to the dominant			
Plus: Chromatic scale starting on F Whole-tone scale starting on F Diminished 7th starting on F	two octaves			
Pentatonic (major) scale starting on E♭ Dominant 7th in the key of D	one octave			

When the examiner requests a **major tonal centre**, the candidate should play in succession:
 	
  The major scale
  The major arpeggio
 	
When the examiner requests a **minor tonal centre**, the candidate should play in succession:
 	
  The melodic minor scale
  The harmonic minor scale
  The minor arpeggio				

or ii) **Orchestral extract** *or* **study**				
See current syllabus for details.				

i) Scales & arpeggios

F major scale (two octaves) – see Treble Recorder Grade 4 page 31

F major arpeggio (two octaves) – see Treble Recorder Grade 4 page 31

F melodic minor scale (two octaves) – see Treble Recorder Grade 5 page 42

F harmonic minor scale (two octaves) – see Treble Recorder Grade 5 page 42

F minor arpeggio (two octaves) – see Treble Recorder Grade 5 page 42

A major scale (to 12th) – see Treble Recorder Grade 5 page 43

A major arpeggio (to 12th) – see Treble Recorder Grade 5 page 43

A melodic minor scale (to 12th) – see Treble Recorder Grade 3 page 22

A harmonic minor scale (to 12th) – see Treble Recorder Grade 3 page 22

A minor arpeggio (to 12th) – see Treble Recorder Grade 3 page 22

Eb major scale (one octave and down to the dominant) – see Treble Recorder Grade 3 page 23

Eb major arpeggio (one octave and down to the dominant) – see Treble Recorder Grade 3 page 23

Eb melodic minor scale (one octave and down to the dominant)

Eb harmonic minor scale (one octave and down to the dominant)

Eb minor arpeggio (one octave and down to the dominant)

Chromatic scale starting on F (two octaves) – see Treble Recorder Grade 5 page 44

Whole-tone scale starting on F (two octaves)

Diminished 7th starting on F (two octaves) – see Treble Recorder Grade 5 page 45

Pentatonic (major) scale starting on Eb (one octave)

Dominant 7th in the key of D (one octave) – see Treble Recorder Grade 5 page 45

Treble Recorder
Grade 7

Candidate to prepare *either* section i) *or* section ii) in full					
either i) **Scales & arpeggios** (from memory) – the examiner will select from the following:					
Candidates should prepare scales and arpeggios from the following tonal centres: C major, C minor Bb major, Bb minor	to 12th	min. tempi: scales: ♩ = 132 arpeggios: ♩. = 69 7ths: ♩ = 116	tongued, slurred *or* staccato-tongued		*mf*
Db major, C# minor E major, E minor	one octave and down to the dominant				
Plus: Chromatic scale starting on Bb Augmented arpeggio starting on C	to 12th				
Whole-tone scale starting on Db Pentatonic (major) scales starting on E and Db Dominant 7ths in the keys of A and Eb Diminished 7th starting on C	one octave				

When the examiner requests a **major tonal centre**, the candidate should play in succession:
 	
  The major scale
  The major arpeggio
 	
When the examiner requests a **minor tonal centre**, the candidate should play in succession:
 	
  The melodic minor scale
  The harmonic minor scale
  The minor arpeggio					

or ii) **Orchestral extract** *or* **study**					
See current syllabus for details.					

i) Scales & arpeggios

C major scale (to 12th) – see Treble Recorder Grade 5 page 43

C major arpeggio (to 12th) – see Treble Recorder Grade 5 page 43

C melodic minor scale (to 12th)

C harmonic minor scale (to 12th)

C minor arpeggio (to 12th)

Bb major scale (to 12th)

Bb major arpeggio (to 12th)

Bb melodic minor scale (to 12th) – see Treble Recorder Grade 5 page 43

Bb harmonic minor scale (to 12th) – see Treble Recorder Grade 5 page 43

Bb minor arpeggio (to 12th) – see Treble Recorder Grade 5 page 43

Db major scale (one octave and down to the dominant) – see Treble Recorder Grade 5 page 44

Db major arpeggio (one octave and down to the dominant) – see Treble Recorder Grade 5 page 44

C# melodic minor scale (one octave and down to the dominant)

C# harmonic minor scale (one octave and down to the dominant)

Treble Recorder Grade 7 continued

C# minor arpeggio (one octave and down to the dominant)

E major scale (one octave and down to the dominant)

E major arpeggio (one octave and down to the dominant)

E melodic minor scale (one octave and down to the dominant) – see Treble Recorder Grade 4 page 32

E harmonic minor scale (one octave and down to the dominant) – see Treble Recorder Grade 4 page 32

E minor arpeggio (one octave and down to the dominant) – see Treble Recorder Grade 4 page 33

Chromatic scale starting on B♭ (to 12th)

Augmented arpeggio starting on C (to 12th)

Whole-tone scale starting on D♭ (one octave)

Pentatonic (major) scale starting on E (one octave)

Pentatonic (major) scale starting on D♭ (one octave)

Dominant 7th in the key of A (one octave)

Dominant 7th in the key of E♭ (one octave)

Diminished 7th starting on C (one octave)

Treble Recorder
Grade 8

Candidate to prepare *either* section i) *or* section ii) in full				
either i) **Scales & arpeggios** (from memory) − the examiner will select from the following:				
Candidates should prepare scales and arpeggios from the following tonal centres: A♭ major	two octaves	min. tempi: scales: ♩ = 132 arpeggios: ♩. = 76 7ths: ♩ = 132	tongued, slurred, staccato-tongued *or* mixed articulation*	*mf*
G♯ minor G major, G minor F♯ major, F♯ minor	to 12th			
D major, D minor B major, B minor	one octave and down to the dominant			
Plus: Pentatonic (major) scale starting on G Diminished 7ths starting on A♭ and G Augmented arpeggios starting on A♭ and G	two octaves			
Chromatic scale starting on F♯	to 12th			
Whole-tone scale starting on F♯ Dominant 7ths in the keys of G and E	one octave			

When the examiner requests a **major tonal centre**, the candidate should play in succession:
 	
  The major scale
  The major arpeggio
 	
When the examiner requests a **minor tonal centre**, the candidate should play in succession:
 	
  The melodic minor scale
  The harmonic minor scale
  The minor arpeggio				

or ii) **Orchestral extract** *or* **study**				
See current syllabus for details.				

*Mixed articulation scales and arpeggios to be prepared with the following articulation:

i) Scales & arpeggios

A♭ major scale (two octaves)

Ab major arpeggio (two octaves)

G# melodic minor scale (to 12th)

G# harmonic minor scale (to 12th)

G# minor arpeggio (to 12th)

G major scale (to 12th) — see Treble Recorder Grade 2 page 14

G major arpeggio (to 12th) — see Treble Recorder Grade 2 page 14

G melodic minor scale (to 12th) — see Treble Recorder Grade 2 page 14

G harmonic minor scale (to 12th) — see Treble Recorder Grade 2 page 14

G minor arpeggio (to 12th) — see Treble Recorder Grade 2 page 15

F# major scale (to 12th)

Treble Recorder Grade 8 continued

F# major arpeggio (to 12th)

F♯ melodic minor scale (to 12th) − see Treble Recorder Grade 5 page 44

F♯ harmonic minor scale (to 12th) − see Treble Recorder Grade 5 page 44

F♯ minor arpeggio (to 12th) − see Treble Recorder Grade 5 page 44

D major scale (one octave and down to the dominant) − see Treble Recorder Grade 4 page 32

D major arpeggio (one octave and down to the dominant) − see Treble Recorder Grade 4 page 32

D melodic minor scale (one octave and down to the dominant) − see Treble Recorder Grade 4 page 32

D harmonic minor scale (one octave and down to the dominant) − see Treble Recorder Grade 4 page 32

D minor arpeggio (one octave and down to the dominant) − see Treble Recorder Grade 4 page 32

B major scale (one octave and down to the dominant)

B major arpeggio (one octave and down to the dominant)

B melodic minor scale (one octave and down to the dominant) − see Descant Recorder Grade 4 page 27

B harmonic minor scale (one octave and down to the dominant) − see Descant Recorder Grade 4 page 27

B minor arpeggio (one octave and down to the dominant) − see Descant Recorder Grade 4 page 28

Pentatonic (major) scale starting on G (two octaves)

Diminished 7th starting on A♭ (two octaves)

Diminished 7th starting on G (two octaves)

Augmented arpeggio starting on A♭ (two octaves)

Augmented arpeggio starting on G (two octaves)

Chromatic scale starting on F♯ (to 12th)

Treble Recorder Grade 8 continued

Whole-tone scale starting on F# (one octave)

Dominant 7th in the key of G (one octave)

Dominant 7th in the key of E (one octave)

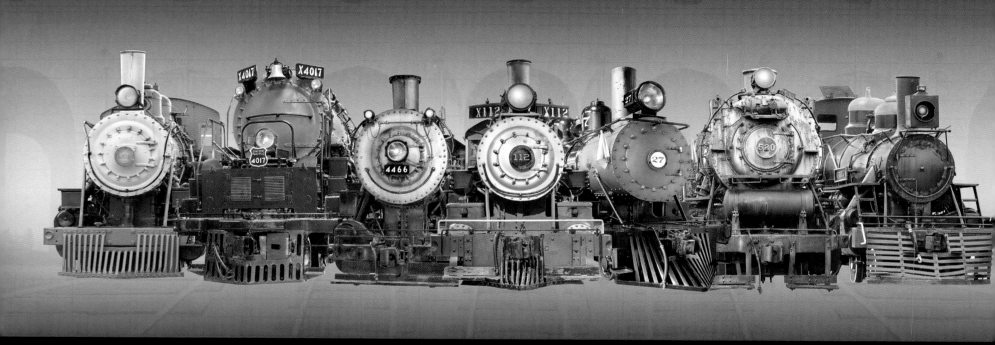

THE ART OF THE LOCOMOTIVE

KEN BOYD

Voyageur
Press

First published in 2014 by Voyageur Press, an imprint of Quarto Publishing Group USA Inc., 400 First Avenue North, Suite 400, Minneapolis, MN 55401 USA

The information in this book is true and complete to the best of our knowledge. All recommendations are made without any guarantee on the part of the author or Publisher, who also disclaims any liability incurred in connection with the use of this data or specific details.

We recognize, further, that some words, model names, and designations mentioned herein are the property of the trademark holder. We use them for identification purposes only. This is not an official publication.

Voyageur Press titles are also available at discounts in bulk quantity for industrial or sales-promotional use. For details write to Special Sales Manager at Quarto Publishing Group USA Inc., 400 First Avenue North, Suite 400, Minneapolis, MN 55401 USA.

To find out more about our books, visit us online at www.voyageurpress.com.

ISBN-13: 978-0-7603-4691-4

Acquisitions Editor: Dennis Pernu
Project Manager: Elizabeth Noll
Art Director: Cindy Samargia Laun
Design and Layout: Simon Larkin

On the front cover: B&O No. 147 (*Thatcher Perkins*)—B&O No. 147, also known as the *Thatcher Perkins* after its designer, was built by B&O in 1863 in the midst of the Civil War. It was one of a series of ten-wheel locomotives with the power necessary for routes through the Appalachian Mountains. It was initially used to move Union troops during the war. It continued as a passenger and freight locomotive in the decades that followed the conflict. Over the years, it was renumbered first as No. 283 and then as No. 117 for the B&O Fair of the Iron Horse in 1927. This locomotive was one of several that were severely damaged when the B&O roundhouse roof collapsed in 2003. It has only recently been meticulously restored by the museum staff and renumbered to the original No. 147. This locomotive is truly beautiful in Indian red, vermillion, dark gray, black, and brass. It is classically outfitted with American flags.

On the back cover: Triple Race— At Cass Scenic Railroad State Park in the mountains of West Virginia, a triple race features Cass Nos. 5, 11, and 6. **(Left) Western Maryland Railway No. 6**—The last Shay locomotive ever produced and the largest Shay in existence. At 162 tons, it is about twice the size of any other Shay at Cass. **(Middle) Cass Scenic Railroad No. 11**—No. 11 is a three-truck Shay locomotive that was built in 1923 by Lima Locomotive Works. **(Right) Mower Lumber Company No. 5**—Built by Lima Locomotive Works in 1905, it is the second-oldest Shay in existence.

On the frontis: Steam locomotives required continuous service and maintenance. Many of the tools and even replacement parts used to service these locomotives were custom-made in railroad blacksmith shops.

On the title page: A composite lineup provides railfans a unique perspective on the history of American steam locomotion.

Printed in China

10 9 8 7 6 5 4 3 2 1

TABLE OF CONTENTS

PREFACE

My journey as a locomotive photographer began quite unintentionally in the late 1970s, first with casual photographs of trains near my home, and then as a more passionate enthusiast. Since that time, I have photographed hundreds of locomotives all across the United States and Canada and some in Europe. My portfolio includes steam, diesel, and electric locomotives and the full range of railroad maintenance, support equipment, and rolling stock for many of the historic American railroads.

My interest in trains started early. My grandfather, born in 1880, worked for the old Seaboard Air Line (SAL) around the turn of the last century. He worked on the route between Atlanta, Georgia and Birmingham, Alabama. He worked mostly in the Wellington, Alabama area, where the SAL east-west lines crossed the Louisville & Nashville (L&N) mineral tracks that ran north and south between Gadsden and Anniston, Alabama. From all accounts, a terrible passenger train collision happened at that crossing sometime in the early 1900s.

As a boy in the 1950s and 1960s, I listened to stories of railroading and trains and travel. My parents and other adult acquaintances at the time grew up in the first half of the twentieth century, through the Great Depression and World War II. They experienced the golden era of the steam-powered locomotive and that important phase of the building of our railroad infrastructure. I heard stories of the Wabash Cannon Ball, the Southerner, the Queen and Crescent, and the dozens of short lines that operated passenger and freight service in the area around my home in northeast Alabama. After World War II, my father worked as a mechanic at a large Air Force munitions depot. He wasn't a train engineer, but he would move the switch engines around for service, and I can remember seeing him sitting up high in the locomotives and leaning forward to see.

From that same era in time, I can recall the old greasy turntables, high trestles, and iron truss bridges that turned to let steamboats pass. I also recall long, spooky tunnels through the mountains near my home, and I was there for the final battle between steam and diesel. This was a great time and place for anyone with an interest in trains, transportation, technology, and mechanical and industrial design. My photos are an attempt to recall, recapture, and share my memories.

I began photographing locomotives and many other subjects after I finished college. I moved to Birmingham to work and continue my education, and I saw that the whole metro area was a grid of train tracks, including a set of very active main lines. These lines still cut the downtown area in half with a series of ancient viaducts and underpasses. In Birmingham, an industrial city, railroading has been a way of life for more than one hundred years. When I moved there, I could hear locomotives in most parts of the city. In addition, the city was home to a very enthusiastic historical railroading society. The society ran steam excursions in the spring and fall and maintained a combination work area and rail equipment junkyard near where I worked and lived. This area was a great resource for early photo experimentation.

Until the mid-1990s, Norfolk Southern Railway maintained steam shops in the nearby Irondale area. On the weekends, rail enthusiasts could view the steam locomotives that were out in the yard for service and restoration work.

My interest in documenting steam locomotives and trains in general grew. From where I worked, up on the side of Red Mountain, I could see the billowing steam as the trains prepared for their excursions in the spring and fall. At first, I clicked pictures of the trains at rest, with some steam and people around. Before long, I got more serious about the process and began to previsualize better images. I scouted the tracks looking for trestles, crossings, and backgrounds that would be in good light when the trains passed. I recall getting out on cold mornings before daylight, driving to rural locations, hiking along the tracks, setting up my tripod and camera, and waiting patiently for a train. My excitement grew as I heard a whistle in the distance, followed by the familiar sound of drive gear and finally a cloud of steam over the trees!

In the early years, my photographs were on 35mm color slide film and occasionally color negative film. As my photography skills improved, I transitioned from color to black and white and from 35mm to larger film cameras and then entirely to digital with the new century.

Photography became my passion, and my photographic eye continued to improve through the 1990s, as did my skill in the darkroom. Around this time, I started teaching darkroom photography classes in the adult education program at the University of Alabama at Birmingham. Through teaching, I learned even more. I printed, toned, hand-colored with oils, and experimented with nineteenth-century processes. The influence of all this is visible in my images today; the best are gathered together here, in *The Art of the Locomotive*.

The Historic B&O Roundhouse.

INTRODUCTION

The photographs I've included in this book are the result of many years of experience, not just as a photographer, but also as a digital artist. Over the years, I've learned how important the basics are in producing quality photographs. Careful planning, good lighting, interesting composition, and sound camera technique are all critical. So is meticulous processing of the final image, whether in the darkroom or on the computer.

My photography today typically involves a high-quality camera or two, a few good lenses, a sturdy tripod, and plenty of digital media. With the advent of the Internet, planning and research became much easier. It is now possible to determine the direction of the sun and see an aerial image of a location on the computer from one thousand miles away. I can plan, choose my equipment, and previsualize an image before I even arrive at a location.

I generally prefer diffused light for locomotives, rather than direct sunlight. Diffused light is predictable and works well for most subjects I photograph. The best ways for me to assure uniform, rich light for my outdoor railroad subjects is to shoot early in the morning, late in the afternoon, or on an overcast day. I also watch the weather and try to use dramatic lighting when it's possible (such as the transitional light on the edge of a storm). Of course, I have to capture some train shots when it is sunny, and in that case, I just do the best I can.

Another lighting scenario that I like occurs on a beautiful day with blue skies and puffy clouds. I set up and take my photographs when the clouds block the sun and temporarily shade the locomotive. With this particular lighting situation, I have the benefit of soft, shadowless light for my subject but a blue sky with nice clouds as my background.

➤ ➤ **Verde Canyon Railroad Electro-Motive Division Diesel-Electric FP7 No. 1510 (built 1953, photographed 2012), Clarkdale, Arizona**—This before-and-after comparison shows how the image has been desaturated and recolored for a more painterly look. The buildings and automobiles in the background have been removed and the foreground and background have been carefully tinted on the computer. The sky was replaced with a sky photographed at the same location a few minutes later in the evening as the light softened and clouds and detail emerged.

⋀ Juanita Shops Electric Class DD-1 Locomotives (built 1911, photographed 2011), Railroad Museum of Pennsylvania, Strasburg, Pennsylvania—This before-and-after comparison provides a good example of the "painterly" look described in the text. The sky has been replaced with a sky from my files that complements the colors and tones in the locomotives. The overall image has been desaturated, recolored, and retouched to bring out the beauty in these massive, amazing locomotives. Notice that the green grass has been toned down to keep the emphasis on the locomotives.

The most difficult lighting I face in photographing historic locomotives is the artificial and often contrasty spotlighting in museums, roundhouses, and sheds. Spotlighting creates uneven light and deep shadows. I bracket extensively, take close-ups of important areas of the locomotive, and plan to take my time and produce a corrected image on the computer. In recent years, digital photography has made difficult lighting much more manageable.

Nighttime locomotive photography, as inspired by O. Winston Link and Richard Steinheimer, is especially fascinating and challenging. I find the results with digital cameras to be generally acceptable and sometimes surprising, whether I'm using existing lights, painting with electronic flash, or adding continuous halogen or even fog and smoke.

To compose my photographs, I not only see the locomotive before me as I shoot on location, but also previsualize how I would like the final image to look. I am constantly thinking about how the image will evolve on my computer.

When I begin shooting, I initially direct my attention to the actual locomotive. First and foremost, I must have a high-quality image or portrait of the locomotive. Will this be the classic three-quarter view, a nose shot, a side view, or something close-up or from a greater distance? I move around and study my options. I make decisions about what to include and what to exclude. I choose the best perspective, in terms of wide-angle or telephoto lens. If I am waiting for the train to arrive, I arrange a frame and set up for the train's arrival. I take as many shots as I can in order to have options later.

➤ ➤ Camden & Amboy Wood-Burning Locomotive *John Bull* (built 1831, photographed 2010), American History Museum, Smithsonian Institute, Washington, D.C.—The *John Bull* is seen above in a cluttered display under harsh exhibit spotlighting near an escalator in the American History Museum. Because of the complexity and intricate detail of this historic locomotive and tender, I decided to go with a simple white background to better reveal the features. The lighting has been carefully evened out by selectively retouching and repainting locomotive details.

◁ ◁ Norfolk Southern General Electric Dash 9-40CW No. 9201 (built 1998, photographed 2011), Sloss Furnaces, Birmingham, Alabama— This image was taken late in the warm glow of the afternoon. From the before-and-after comparison, it is obvious that a more dramatic sky has been inserted. Historic Sloss Furnaces in the distance has been enlarged for emphasis, and other locomotives and railcars have been included from separate exposures. Finally, utility poles, shadows, highlights, and other elements have been edited extensively.

I have reviewed my strategy for planning, lighting, and composition, but I think what really makes my locomotive images unique is my post-processing. My personal vision for locomotive photography has evolved with time and practice and is now pretty well defined. In words adapted from Norman Rockwell: my intention is to show a locomotive as I would *like* it to be, with as much feeling and drama as possible. I aim for an idealized and sometimes romantic presentation. This has become my approach and my philosophy for photography: a simple, clean, orderly, and optimistic representation of my subject.

To put this philosophy into practice, I am keenly aware of the background, foreground, and other elements of the overall composition and how these may affect my locomotive image and the mood invoked. As I am composing and recording a locomotive image, I am continually assessing my options about the background and everything I see in front of the camera and around the immediate area. Locomotives are often in cluttered, photographically chaotic settings; outdoors in unflattering light; or in crowded museum locations with difficult interior lighting. I ask myself how I can best make the situation work for this particular image and what can I do to refine the situation either now or on the computer later.

Because the background tells so much of a locomotive's story, it has to be right. The background not only becomes the setting for the image, but also establishes the mood and tone by providing clues about what was going on when I photographed the locomotive. Because I prefer orderly, uncomplicated compositions, the background must contrast well with the locomotive and not be overly distracting. Locomotives themselves are very intricate and complex, and a simple background can make the locomotive more distinct. On another level, the background must also add to the beauty and feeling of the composition.

Sometimes I replace the real background entirely. The replacement background must come from somewhere, and my first choice is a background from a slightly different angle or view at the location where I photographed the locomotive. This background would most likely be a simpler and cleaner scene with the same lighting and some clues about the location. Another option is a basic skyline, hillside, or woodland scene that complements the locomotive without providing misleading information. Over time, I have built a library of dramatic sky and cloud images and images of rural, urban, and hillside scenes as well as stone walls and other structures often found around stations and yards. I use this collection of images as a resource for possible use as backgrounds in my locomotive photographs.

I occasionally resort to a plain and almost studio-looking background that presents the locomotive in a very simple and straightforward manner. I most often apply this technique for images of very old, historic, and classic locomotives.

Along with the background, I often work extensively in the foreground to assure emphasis on the locomotive and to enhance the overall image. The foreground provides the foundation for the image and is extremely important in the overall composition. My work in foregrounds may involve adding, moving, or replacing elements and overlaying or retouching to provide a better overall sense of the setting. When I digitally replace entire foregrounds, I take great care to maintain proper perspective. Replacing foregrounds is more difficult digitally than replacing backgrounds. Individual foreground elements I may remove or replace are modern sidewalks, asphalt, signs, poles, garbage cans, parts of vehicles, parking meters, fences, and unsightly clutter—any items that are inconsistent with my composition and my idealized-image philosophy. This kind of work can totally transform an image.

Post-processing is an exciting step for me. This is the most creative part of my work. It is an opportunity to realize my vision. I use the computer monitor as a canvas. I begin by reviewing my images and making adjustments and refinements to the locomotives. I even out the lighting, enhance highlights and shadows, add color, build in details, and generally make the locomotive look more idealized.

In terms of color, my locomotive photography is often described as "painterly." This means that the images look somewhat more like paintings than traditional photographs. This is the aspect of my photography that generates the most interest and discussion.

I often introduce at least some additional color or enhance the existing color in my images. My colors are usually—though not always—muted and subtle, but they are extremely important to the composition and design. Sometimes I actually subdue the colors in the original image as shot and then add my own colors. I use color to create emphasis and to guide the viewer to the point of interest, which may be the headlight, a driver, the cab, or something else. This technique makes the photograph more powerful.

I treat and edit dark and light areas and details of the image in the same way I manage color. I can brighten up many images by working in the existing highlights and shadows. I often deepen the shadows and brighten the highlights, much as I would add or subdue colors. Alternatively, I may open shadows to reveal detail hidden in the dark tones.

➤ ➤ **Tennessee Valley Railroad Baldwin-Lima-Hamilton Coal-Fired Steam Locomotive No. 610 (built 1952, photographed 2005), Tennessee Valley Railroad Museum, Chattanooga, Tennessee**—This image was taken in the yard at the Tennessee Valley Railroad Museum while the locomotive was being serviced after a run. The background has been replaced with a scene typical of a hillside from the lower Appalachian Mountains. The column of steam and smoke was photographed a few minutes earlier as the locomotive pulled into the yard.

◁ ◁ Union Pacific Alco Big Boy Coal-Fired Steam Locomotive No. 4012 (built 1941, photographed 2013), Steamtown, Scranton, Pennsylvania— The images on the top are shown as they were shot under overcast conditions in the yard area. On the bottom, I decided to go with a view that shows both the massive façade of the locomotive and the incredible centipede tender in a single image. The background is from a scene reminiscent of the Wasatch Range where this locomotive logged more than a million miles. The foreground has been reworked and tracks have been transformed as necessary. Every detail of the locomotive and tender has been carefully retouched.

I treat black-and-white and sepia images with equal attention to detail. But instead of painting in colors, I paint with black, white, and shades of gray or sepia taken from the images. Why choose black and white in a digital environment when color is available and really costs no more? Well, first of all, the colors in the scene may be unattractive or inharmonious within the image, or the colors may make the scene appear to be too busy and complicated. If the composition is very strong and clean, the image may simply look better in black and white. For a vintage or historic look, sepia or even a blue-toned image may be a good option.

I find digital image editing to be thoroughly engaging. My goal is perfection in the final image—I want it to be simple, clean, and eye-catching. Using the teachings of Jerry Uelsmann (the father of photographic collage, montage, and combined imaging), I have become comfortable with replacing a washed-out sky with a colorful sky, moving buildings, deleting fences, correcting a scene for a period look, or even completely eliminating the foreground and background.

As my locomotive photography has evolved over the last few years, I have gradually introduced creative digital effects software to help me produce the best possible images of my locomotives. This software allows me to vary the look of my photographs and produce a more diverse portfolio of locomotive images. Over time and with experimentation, I have come to appreciate the creative power of digital editing software. This software allows me to transform an image; the results can be seen in some of my more recent work.

Photography is indeed my passion and joy. And to me, locomotives are almost unrivaled as an awe-inspiring subject. From their power and classic presence to the sounds and sights that come with them—blasting steam, chugging smoke, whistles, bells, and lights—these machines awaken an imaginative and visionary spirit in all who experience them. The array of designs, color schemes, geographic setting, and grand history inspires many photographers to record railroading images and many more to share in an appreciation of the locomotive.

As we progress through the twenty-first century, we will witness the ongoing introduction of new imaging tools. It will be exciting to participate in this extraordinary time for photography—especially for photography of the locomotive.

CHAPTER 1

THE EARLY YEARS (1820–1899)

The story of the locomotive in America begins in the 1820s and 1830s. Although the steam engine and the locomotive were first developed in Europe, the technology quickly found its way to America.

In 1825, Colonel John Stevens, the "father of the American railroads," successfully built and operated a simple locomotive he called the Steam Waggon at his estate in New Jersey. This was an experiment and not a commercial venture, but it demonstrated that steam-powered rail transportation was possible.

Peter Cooper introduced the first really successful American locomotive, the *Tom Thumb*, in 1830. The *Tom Thumb* lost its famous race to a horse when it threw a drive belt, but in spite of that, it proved to American business interests that the future of transportation was the locomotive. Several locomotive designs were tested in the early 1830s. These early designs included the *Best Friend of Charleston*, the *York*, the *Atlantic*, and the *John Bull*. After just a few more years, the quaint vertical boiler design of these locomotives gave way to the familiar horizontal boiler, beginning with the *Lafayette*, to allow for larger and more powerful machines.

Locomotive design and function continued to evolve. Beautifully elegant locomotives such as the *Pioneer*, the *Daniel Nason*, the *William Crooks*, the *Governor Stanford*, the *C. P. Huntington*, and the *Thatcher Perkins* are examples of the phenomenal development and evolution of the technology over just a few decades. In 1835 fewer than two hundred locomotives existed in America, but by 1880 the number approached forty thousand!

Unfortunately, only a few of our earliest locomotives remain. Working replicas have been produced for some of the very early designs, and these replicas are now a century old. Join me now to marvel at these remaining early locomotives and consider how they enriched our lives and changed the course of American history.

Λ **John Stevens Steam Waggon (Replica)**— Stevens is generally considered to be the father of the American railroad. Stevens served under George Washington during the American Revolution and subsequently experimented with steamboat designs. But it was his Steam Waggon that introduced the locomotive to North America. In 1825 he set up a circular track on his estate in Hoboken, New Jersey. He operated his invention as a demonstration through 1826 and 1827. For the demonstration, passengers rode on the Steam Waggon with Stevens and the boiler, not in trailing cars as with later trains. Stevens' locomotive, which was basically a wagon with a small steam engine and probably cog wheels without flanges, could attain speeds of up to about 12 miles per hour with several passengers onboard. The original vertical wood-burning boiler—but not the actual locomotive—is preserved at the Smithsonian Institution in Washington D. C. A 1928 replica of the locomotive is on display at the Museum of Science and Industry in Chicago, Illinois. A second replica is preserved at the Railroad Museum of Pennsylvania.

◄ *Tom Thumb* (Replica)—The *Tom Thumb* is one of the most famous of all locomotives, and most children learn about it in school. American industrialist Peter Cooper designed and constructed this locomotive in 1830 as a demonstration for what would become the Baltimore & Ohio Railroad (B&O). The locomotive was a 2-2-0 design with vertical cylinders and a vertical boiler that operated on anthracite coal. The *Tom Thumb* is most famous for losing a race to a horse when its blower belt slipped off a pulley; it lost power and the horse won. Despite the outcome of the race, this demonstration convinced business interests that steam engines offered potential on the rails. B&O built a replica of the original *Tom Thumb* in 1927. It is now displayed at the B&O Railroad Museum. Although this replica was carefully designed, it is thought to vary considerably from the original.

➤ *Best Friend of Charleston* (Replica)—
This visually charming 0-4-0 locomotive is an operable 1928 replica of a locomotive built for the South Carolina Canal and Railroad Company by West Point Foundry in 1830. The original *Best Friend of Charleston* pulled several cars and was capable of speeds up to 15 to 20 miles per hour. It provided regular passenger service in Charleston, South Carolina until it suffered a boiler explosion in 1831. The boiler exploded after a fireman wired the pressure relief valve shut! The replica, in classic Southern Railway green and gold, is currently on loan from the city of Charleston to Norfolk Southern Railway. It is on display at the company office building in Atlanta. A second replica can be seen at the South Carolina State Museum in Columbia.

➤➤ *John Bull*—This classically beautiful wood-burning locomotive has great historical significance in the United States. It was built in England and assembled in Pennsylvania. Camden & Amboy Railroad (C&A) of New Jersey first operated the *John Bull* in 1831 and continued to operate it over the next thirty-five years. The Pennsylvania Railroad acquired the *John Bull* in 1871 and refurbished it. It operated most recently in 1981. It is the world's oldest operable self-propelled vehicle, and it is on display in the National Museum of American History at the Smithsonian Institution. This locomotive became the inspiration for Matthias Baldwin, the founder of Baldwin Locomotive Works, the world's largest producer of steam locomotives. Baldwin's company produced more than seventy thousand locomotives before ending operations in 1956.

**◄◄ *Pennsylvania Railroad No. 1*
(Replica)**—*The Pennsylvania Railroad
No. 1* is a 1939 replica of the 1831 C&A
John Bull with a taller chimney and a few
other cosmetic and technical refinements.
The locomotive is on display at the Railroad
Museum of Pennsylvania along with C&A
coach No. 1 from 1836, the second-oldest
passenger coach in the United States.
Pennsylvania Railroad built the replica
locomotive to replace the original *John Bull*
at the World's Fair in 1940. Although the
original *John Bull* was still operable, and
the Pennsylvania Railroad had continued to
use it occasionally, the company decided
to produce a replica and no longer risk
damage to the original *John Bull*. After
the World's Fair and other events over the
next few decades, *Pennsylvania Railroad
No. 1* sat for years in the weather and
deteriorated. It was cosmetically restored
in 1982 and 1983 but currently is not
certified for operation, because it does not
comply with modern steam boiler safety
certification regulations.

◄ *York* (Replica)—The original 0-4-0
coal-fired *York* was the first locomotive
to be operated by B&O. The *York's* design
was somewhat similar to that of the *Tom
Thumb*. It used two vertical cylinders
for power. It was built by Phineas Davis
in York, Pennsylvania, in 1831 as one of
three designs tested by B&O. B&O built a
replica in 1927 at its Mount Clare Shops and
demonstrated the replica at the Fair of the
Iron Horse that same year. The replica later
appeared at the Chicago World's Fair in
1933 and 1934. The replica is preserved in
beautiful condition at Chicago's Museum of
Science and Industry.

➤ *Lafayette* (**Replica**)—In 1837 the Norris Locomotive Works in Philadelphia, Pennsylvania built the 4-2-0 *Lafayette* locomotive for B&O. The horizontal boiler design of this locomotive established a configuration that would be followed around the world until the end of the steam era more than one hundred years later. The horizontal boiler and linkages with a trailing tender car allowed locomotives to move faster and more efficiently than earlier, smaller, vertical-boiler designs could. Also, the horizontal cylinders were less damaging to rails than the pounding of vertical cylinders. A 1927 replica, which is still generally considered operable, is on display in superb cosmetic condition at the B&O Railroad Museum.

➤ ➤ *Atlantic* (**Replica**)—In 1832, after the design of the *York* was selected by B&O, Phineas Davis built the *Atlantic*, his second locomotive. This was a standard gauge, 0-4-0, anthracite coal–fired locomotive with a vertical boiler and two cylinders. Because of the *Atlantic's* success, twenty additional locomotives of a similar design were built. The original *Atlantic* was scrapped in 1835, but a beautiful replica was built in 1892 and is now on display with period cars in the roundhouse at the B&O Railroad Museum.

➤ **B&O No. 57 (*Memnon*)**— Newcastle Manufacturing Company built this 0-8-0 locomotive, also known as the the *Old War Horse*, in 1848. It is one of the oldest surviving American freight locomotives. The *Memnon* has been altered very little from its 1848 design, is in immaculate condition, and is an extremely important example of the rare mid-1800s locomotive. It was used to pull long coal and passenger trains. It burned coal, whereas most engines of that day burned wood. It is housed at the magnificent B&O Railroad Museum in Baltimore, where the historic railroad was organized in 1827. A 2003 roundhouse roof collapse damaged the *Memnon*. Restoration was completed in 2008.

◄ **The *Pioneer***—The *Pioneer* is one of the most historically significant original locomotives in the world. Union Works of South Boston, Massachusetts built the *Pioneer* in 1851. It is a 2-2-2 tank design with no tender for additional coal and water. Cumberland Valley Railroad owned and operated the locomotive and used it for passenger service. During the Civil War, the engine carried supplies and troops for the Union army. After the war, the *Pioneer* remained in service until 1901, when it began a second career as an exhibit for fairs and exhibitions around the country. Pennsylvania Railroad donated the *Pioneer* to the Smithsonian Institution in 1961. In 2010, the National Museum of American History and the B&O Railroad Museum began an extensive restoration of the engine, which is now complete.

⮞ Boston & Providence Railroad No. 17 (*Daniel Nason*)—The *Daniel Nason* is among the most treasured industrial artifacts of the United States. This locomotive was built in Boston, Massachusetts by Roxbury Locomotive Works between 1858 and 1863. Although the 4-4-0 wheel arrangement was popular during this era, this is the only surviving locomotive with the cylinders and main driving rods located inside the locomotive frame. The *Daniel Nason* was one of twenty-eight locomotives produced under the direction of George Griggs, generally considered one of the greatest locomotive designers in U.S. history. It has been displayed in several major exhibits, including the 1893 World's Columbian Exposition in Chicago and the 1939–1940 World's Fair in New York. For a time the *Daniel Nason* was part of the Purdue University collection. It was donated to the Museum of Transportation in Saint Louis, Missouri in 1982. The Boston & Providence Railroad (B&P) was an early railroad in New England. It became part of the New York, New Haven & Hartford Railroad and is now a component of the Amtrak Northeast Corridor.

⮞⮞ (Left) Northern Pacific Railway No. 1 (*Minnetonka*)—This unique locomotive is commonly known as the *Minnetonka*. It is an 1870 Smith & Porter 0-4-0T wood burner. It was one of the first four steam locomotives purchased by Northern Pacific for use during the construction of the Northern Pacific main line as the railroad pushed to connect Puget Sound with the Great Lakes. The *Minnetonka* was shipped in parts around Cape Horn and reassembled at Kalama, Washington, in about 1871. This small engine was later used in logging work in the northwestern United States before finding a final home in Minnesota. It is on display alongside the *William Crooks* at the Lake Superior Railroad Museum. **(Right) Great Northern Railway No. 1 (*William Crooks*)**—This locomotive is also known as the *William Crooks*. It is named after the locomotive's original chief engineer. It is a beautiful, elaborately decorated, vintage 4-4-0, American design. It was built in 1861, during the Civil War, by the New Jersey Locomotive & Machine Company at Paterson, New Jersey. It became the first locomotive in the state of Minnesota—and the northwestern United States—and provided passenger service in and around Saint Paul. It has been carefully preserved over the years, first by Saint Paul & Pacific Railroad and subsequently by Great Northern Railway. The *William Crooks* can be seen at the Lake Superior Railroad Museum in Duluth, Minnesota. It weighs about 40 tons, is 51 feet in length, and has 63-inch drivers.

Stockton Terminal & Eastern No. 1—
This impressive locomotive operated almost continuously from 1864 until 1953. It features a classic American 4-4-0 wheel configuration and is now on display at the Travel Town Museum in Los Angeles, California. The oil-burning engine was built by Norris Locomotive Works, which was the largest manufacturer of locomotives in the United States and perhaps the world through the mid-1800s. Norris produced almost one thousand locomotives between 1832 and 1866, with some going to Europe. The company's quality and production fell during the Civil War, and Norris went out of business in 1866.

Central Pacific Railroad No. 1 (*Governor Stanford*)—This was the Central Pacific Railroad's first locomotive. It is popularly known as the *Governor Stanford*, after Leland Stanford, the first president of the railroad and a former governor of California. The beautiful 40-ton, wood-burning 4-4-0 locomotive was built during the Civil War in 1862 by Norris Locomotive Works. It was sailed disassembled around South America for delivery in California. The *Governor Stanford* was used for passenger and freight service and even worked in the construction of the First Transcontinental Railroad. It is now displayed in immaculate 1899 condition at the California State Railroad Museum in Sacramento. The original 1862 condition was not possible as part of the restoration, because the boiler and cylinders had been rebuilt and enlarged in 1878. The locomotive was donated to Stanford University after it retired in 1895. It was displayed, then stored, then disassembled, then reassembled, and displayed again while in the university's possession. When the university needed space, it donated the locomotive to the state railway and locomotive society, which became the California State Railroad Museum. *Courtesy California State Parks*

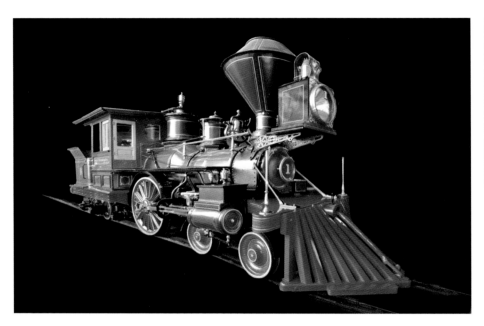

Southern Pacific Railroad No. 1 (C. P. Huntington)—The *C. P. Huntington* is a very famous locomotive in Northern California. For years it was the symbol for the Southern Pacific Railroad and made numerous promotional appearances for the railroad. It was later displayed at the old state fairgrounds and then placed in the Central Pacific Station in Old Sacramento. The *C. P. Huntington* was refurbished in 1970 at the Sacramento railroad shops. It is now on prominent display in beautiful 1914 condition at the spectacular California State Railroad Museum, where it also forms part of the museum logo. Danforth, Cooke & Company of New Jersey built the 4-2-4 oil-burner locomotive with rear tender for the Central Pacific Railroad in 1863 and shipped it from New York around Cape Horn to San Francisco, California, in 1864. Southern Pacific purchased the *C. P. Huntington* in 1871. Southern Pacific used the locomotive for everything from right-of-way weed burning to display and exposition. *Courtesy California State Parks*

Santa Cruz Railroad No. 3 (*Jupiter*)— This beautifully detailed, narrow gauge, 4-4-0, wood-burning, American-style locomotive was built by Baldwin Locomotive Works in 1876 for Santa Cruz Railroad Company in California. It is commonly known as the *Jupiter*, but it should not be confused with the *Jupiter* of transcontinental railroad fame. A number of early American locomotives were named *Jupiter*. No. 3 was used in California for light freight, agriculture, and passenger work, and in 1883 it was sold to International Railway of Central America in Guatemala. There it was used to transport bananas, coffee, and passengers until 1960. The locomotive was then purchased for a children's park in Washington, D.C. in the late 1960s. John White, curator at the Smithsonian Institution, persuaded the owners to donate the locomotive to the Smithsonian for the 1976 centennial celebration. White and John Stine and a team restored the *Jupiter* essentially to original Baldwin specifications, including the paint and the beautiful walnut cab. The locomotive is now on display in the National Museum of American History.

◄ **North Pacific Coast Railroad No. 12
(*The Sonoma*)**— Baldwin Locomotive Works
built this narrow gauge, 4-4-0, oil-fired
locomotive in 1876. It was used for both
passenger and freight service in Marin and
Sonoma counties north of San Francisco
until it was sold to Nevada Central Railroad
in 1879. There it worked until 1938, when
the railroad went bankrupt. *The Sonoma*
was next outfitted to look much like the
Central Pacific Jupiter. It was used in
transcontinental railroad reenactments
in San Francisco until 1940. After years of
storage, No. 12 was donated to the California
State Railroad Museum in 1978. There it was
restored and is now displayed in beautiful
and essentially original condition. *Courtesy
California State Parks*

◀ **Virginia & Truckee Railroad No. 11 (*The Reno*)**—This historic locomotive is commonly known as the *Reno No. 11*, although in recent years it has been temporarily renamed for various movie roles. *The Reno* is a 4-4-0 wood burner and is one of the most famous locomotives in the world. Baldwin Locomotive Works built *The Reno* in 1872. It was originally owned and operated by the Virginia & Truckee Railroad. *The Reno* was and is a picturesque western locomotive that hauled more than $400 million in gold and silver from the Comstock Lode. The locomotive also carried several American icons, including President Ulysses S. Grant, President Theodore Roosevelt, Union General William Tecumseh Sherman, and circus legend P. T. Barnum. It can be seen and enjoyed at the historic Old Tucson Studios in a scenic, mountainous desert region near Tucson, Arizona, where it has undergone some cosmetic restoration in recent years. It has appeared in more than one hundred films at Old Tucson, including movies starring John Wayne, Katherine Hepburn, Paul Newman, Barbara Stanwyck, and Clint Eastwood.

➤ **Nevada Short Line No. 1**—Nevada Short Line No. 1 is a Baldwin-built, narrow gauge, 2-6-0 Mogul-type locomotive that dates from 1879. The locomotive was originally ordered by the Hobart Mills Company and was sold to the Nevada Short Line Railway in August 1913. It was one of two locomotives owned by the railroad, which operated in the silver mining country of Nevada. The locomotive and rolling stock, which are in excellent condition, can be experienced in an attractive display above the main floor at the California State Railroad Museum. (*Courtesy California State Parks*)

◁ **Clinchfield Railroad No. 1**—This valuable locomotive was built in 1882 in Logansport, Indiana in the shops of the Columbus, Chicago & Indiana Central Railway (CC&IC). *The Clinchfield* operated in the Carolinas, Tennessee, Kentucky, and Virginia, primarily Appalachian regions. It was originally known as CC&IC No. 423 and later as Black Mountain No. 1. It is a standard gauge, 2-6-0, coal-fired, Mogul-type locomotive that became part of the collection at the B&O Railroad Museum in 1979. It is fully restored cosmetically but not mechanically. Some interest has been expressed in returning the locomotive to Erwin, Tennessee. The Clinchfield Railroad is now part of CSX Transportation.

➤ Denver, South Park & Pacific Railroad No. 191—This is the oldest authentic locomotive in the state of Colorado, a state with many remarkable steam locomotives. It was built in 1880 by Baldwin Locomotive Works as a 2-8-0, coal-fired, narrow gauge engine. The locomotive was used in mining operations in central Colorado during and after the mineral boom. Denver, South Park & Pacific (DSP&P) later became part of the Colorado & Southern Railway. This historic locomotive can be seen and appreciated at the extensive Colorado Railroad Museum in Golden, Colorado.

◁ Denver & Rio Grande Western Railroad No. 683—No. 683 is a 2-8-0, standard gauge, coal-fired locomotive built in 1890 by Baldwin Locomotive Works. The locomotive has 47-inch drivers and is on prominent display along with No. 191 at the outstanding Colorado Railroad Museum.

◀ Philadelphia & Reading Railroad Company *Black Diamond*—Although the *Black Diamond* may look like a trolley car, streetcar, or early steam dummy, it is actually a coal-fired, 2-2-2T locomotive that was used by railroad officers, managers, and foremen to inspect construction and railroad projects for the Philadelphia & Reading. The *Black Diamond* was built in 1889 by Baldwin Locomotive Works and is beautifully detailed with walnut woodwork, nickel-plated hardware, and French plate glass. It has leather seating for about 8 and a tight area for a crew of two. This locomotive is one of more than 90 inspection locomotives that operated in the U.S. but may be the only surviving example. It retired in 1908 and was owned by the Pennsylvania Reading Coal and Iron Company (P&R C&I Co.) until 1949. The *Black Diamond* was purchased by the National Museum of Transportation in St. Louis in 1979. It was restored in the 1930s by Reading and again in 2011 at the museum, where it is displayed under cover.

▶ Manitou & Pikes Peak Railway No. 1—This was the first locomotive to be used for climbing Pikes Peak from Manitou Springs in central Colorado. It reached the 14,110-foot Pikes Peak summit for the first time in 1891. Baldwin Locomotive Works built the locomotive. It is a coal-fired, cog-type locomotive designed to climb the 16-percent grade on the mountain. The railroad was started by the Simmons family, who also founded the Beautyrest Mattress Company. This locomotive can be examined at the Colorado Railroad Museum.

➤ **The Historic B&O Roundhouse**—Unlike most roundhouses, the B&O roundhouse forms a complete 360-degree circle, with the turntable in the center of the building. This is a unique design, and with its hardwood flooring, the facility has an almost cathedral-like elegance. The roundhouse was built in 1884 in the midst of the expansive Mount Clare Shops at Camden Yards. The B&O Railroad Museum opened in the roundhouse in 1953. Today it displays a collection of the most historic locomotives in North America. This image features the 1856 *William Mason* on the left and the 1848 *Memnon* on the right. During a heavy snowstorm in early 2003, the roundhouse roof collapsed and damaged several invaluable locomotives and other equipment. The roundhouse closed and did not reopen until late 2004. Restoration of the damaged equipment has been a tedious and lengthy process.

➤ ➤ **Sierra Railway No. 3**—Sierra Railway No. 3 is an oil-burning, 4-6-0 design built by the Rogers Locomotive and Machine Works of Paterson, New Jersey in 1891. The locomotive is part of the heritage collection at Railtown 1897 State Historic Park, which is in turn part of the California State Railroad Museum and state park system. With its classic styling, No. 3 is often called the "movie star locomotive." It is the most photographed locomotive in the world. It has appeared in more movies and television shows than any other locomotive, including the *Reno 11*, another very popular movie locomotive. Movie and television credits include *Back to the Future Part III*, *The Unforgiven*, *Bad Girls*, *The Virginian*, *Bonanza*, *Little House on the Prairie*, *Gunsmoke*, *Lassie*, *Death Valley Days*, *Rawhide*, and *The Great Race*. The locomotive was built for the Prescott & Arizona Central Railway, but that railroad went bankrupt in 1893, and No. 3 was relocated to Jamestown, California. It was designed to burn wood or coal but was later converted to burn oil. Like a number of other historic American steam locomotives, No. 3 was taken out of service to conform with boiler safety standards, but it has undergone a complete restoration to its 1929 configuration. It officially returned to service in 2010 at Railtown 1897 State Historic Park.

◄ Northern Pacific Railway No. 927—
The 0-6-0 No. 927 was built in 1896 by Baldwin Locomotive Works and is one of five L-series Northern Pacific engines that have been preserved. No. 927 can be seen in the beautiful rural setting of the Iron Horse Central Railroad Museum in Chisago City, Minnesota.

➤ Georgia Railroad No. 724—This was the last conventional steam locomotive to operate in the Saint Louis area. It is an 1896, 0-6-0, coal-fired locomotive produced by Baldwin Locomotive Works. It was used to switch hopper cars at a gravel plant until it retired in 1963. No. 724 is on display at the Museum of Transportation, where it has been color-coded to provide an educational explanation of how a steam locomotive works.

➤ ➤ Railroad Handcar Pump-operated handcars such as this example at Railtown 1897 State Historic Park were used in railroading around the world as maintenance, inspection, and even passenger vehicles. They date from as early as the 1850s and 1860s. Most were phased out in the early twentieth century as motorized railcars, or speeders, were introduced. This model features metal flanged wheels, foot brakes, and a classic hand pump that can be operated by four riders. Sometimes called a gandy dancers, handcars are often shown in comedic movie and television scenes with locomotives in chase, especially in older films.

CHAPTER 2

THE GOLDEN ERA (1900–1930)

By the dawn of the twentieth century, passenger and the freight trains had become a way of life across the continent. Americans were captivated by the locomotive and rail travel. The railroads experienced steady growth in passengers and freight movement. In 1920, rail travel in the United States peaked at 1.2 billion passengers! As the number of passengers and the tons of freight increased, the locomotive continued to evolve.

The variety in steam locomotive designs, sizes, wheel arrangements, chimney styles, and other features grew as the railroads and the locomotive manufacturers competed for market share. The demand for larger and faster locomotives drove innovation. Bigger boilers, higher pressures, more wheels and axles, multiple cylinders, and so on were all part of a technology revolution. Each successive model and development brought significant changes in railroad technology.

Almost from the beginning—and certainly after the Civil War—three large and successful companies dominated the locomotive market. The largest of these was the Baldwin Locomotive Works. American Locomotive Company, formed from about a half-dozen smaller companies across the eastern United States and Canada, was also a very large, successful manufacturer for many years. Lima Locomotive Works in Lima, Ohio, was the third-largest company. It produced a number of innovative and popular designs. Smaller producers included Rogers Locomotive and Machine Works, Montreal Locomotive Works, H. K. Porter, Brooks Locomotive Works, Davenport Locomotive Works, Cooke Locomotive and Machine Works, Vulcan Iron Works, New Jersey Locomotive and Machine Company, Rhode Island Locomotive Works, Richmond Locomotive Works, and Norris Locomotive Works. Over time, other companies bought up these smaller manufacturers, or they went out of business.

➤ ➤ **The Old West by Rail**—For anyone who grew up in the 1950s and 1960s and enjoyed watching Westerns on television and at the movies, this image will bring back fond memories. More significantly, anyone interested in American history will understand that it was the locomotive and the railroad that opened the West to development from the mid-1800s through the early 1900s. With the completion of the transcontinental railroads, rapid travel and transport of goods from coast to coast was possible.

◄ ◄ **Pacific Electric No. 1544**—Pacific Electric No. 1544 is a very unique older electric locomotive that is affectionately known as the *Electra*. It was built in 1902 for use in the San Francisco area. Unfortunately, it drew so much power when it operated that streetcars and other equipment on the same line could barely move. So *Electra* was often used at night and in other off-peak periods.

In later life, *Electra* traveled south and was employed in subway tunnel construction under Los Angeles, where the clean electric technology was welcomed as an alternative to steam. The unusual sloped front and rear sections of the locomotive were actually taken from steam locomotive tenders! No. 1544 is now on display in its distinctive red coloring at the Travel Town Museum.

Λ **Southern Railway No. 630**—This coal-fired locomotive was built in 1904 by American Locomotive Company in Richmond, Virginia for Southern Railway. The wheel arrangement is 2-8-0, which is referred to as a Consolidation, and at Southern Railway as a Ks-1 class locomotive. No. 630 worked at Southern Railway in freight service, including short haul and large yard work, until 1952 when it was retired and sold. In 1967, it was traded back to Southern Railway, underwent some restoration, and was used in steam excursions until 1983, when it was retired

again. After being leased and loaned for a number of years, the locomotive was donated to the Tennessee Valley Railroad Museum in 1999. At the museum, it underwent a decade-long extensive restoration, including frame and drive-gear rework, and returned to excursion service in 2011. Since that time, the locomotive has been used by the museum around Chattanooga, Tennessee. It has also become part of Norfolk Southern Railway's 21st Century Steam Program with excursions in Alabama, North Carolina, and Virginia, as well as across Tennessee.

➤ T. R. Miller Mill Company No. 12—
This locomotive is of the relatively
unusual 2-4-2T Columbian design. It was
manufactured by Baldwin Locomotive
Works in 1904 and is standard gauge.
No. 12 is preserved in beautiful display
condition at the Historic Pensacola Village
in Florida. It was used at the T. R. Miller
lumber mill and telephone pole treatment
plant north of Pensacola, Florida and
Mobile, Alabama.

**➤ ➤ Pennsylvania Railroad No.
1223**—No. 1223 is a stunning example of
a "modern" 4-4-0 American locomotive. It
was built as a high-speed passenger engine
with tall driving wheels in Pennsylvania
Railroad's Juniata Shops in Altoona in
1905. Later in life, the tall 68-inch drivers
were replaced with smaller wheels. Other
modification were made for freight work.
No. 1223 appeared in the 1969 movie
Hello, Dolly! with Barbara Streisand and
Walter Matthau in a sequence of glamorous
cinematography along the Hudson River.
This locomotive was listed on the National
Register of Historic Places in 1979. It sits on
prominent static display at the Railroad
Museum of Pennsylvania in Strasburg,
near Lancaster. The firebox does not meet
the current stringent Federal Railroad
Administration regulations for operation.

◄ ◄ **Triple Race**—Racing and competition have been a part of human history since the dawn of civilization. From Olympic athletics and chariots to automobiles, boats, and planes, racing has provided entertainment. Racing locomotives is part of this heritage. At Cass Scenic Railroad State Park in the mountains of West Virginia, the tracks near the station are perfect for seeing who is most skilled and who has the best-tuned equipment. This triple race features Cass Nos. 5, 11, and 6. **(Left) Western Maryland Railway No. 6**—This amazing three-truck machine was the last Shay locomotive ever produced and is the largest Shay in existence. Lima Locomotive Works designed and built the powerful engine for Western Maryland's coal-hauling service on a steep 9-percent grade, but the locomotive was used for only about four years on this run. It was built in 1945, stored for twenty-six years at the B&O Railroad Museum, and then shipped to Cass Scenic Railroad State Park in 1981. At 162 tons, it is about twice the size of any other Shay at Cass. **(Middle) Cass Scenic Railroad No. 11**—No. 11 is a three-truck Shay locomotive that was built in 1923 by Lima Locomotive Works. It has been used both as a logger and as a common carrier. No. 11 is the second-largest Shay at Cass. **(Right) Mower Lumber Company No. 5**—This three-truck Shay locomotive was built by Lima Locomotive Works in 1905 and it has now been in operation for more than one hundred years, making it one of the oldest engines in the world in continuous service on its original line. It is the second-oldest Shay in existence.

⋀ Shay Locomotive Driveshaft and Gearing— Ephraim Shay developed and patented the Shay locomotives, and Lima Locomotive Works built them. They have conventional fireboxes and boilers but operate through a side-mounted driveshaft technology rather than with the familiar piston linkage driver design of most steam locomotives. Shays can climb the steepest grades, pull very heavy loads, make hairpin turns, and run on temporary track. They are designed so that all wheels pull, including the wheels on the tender. Shay locomotives were the most popular of the geared steam locomotives, but the competing Heisler and Climax designs were also fairly common.

Shays at Cass—The Cass Scenic Railroad is an outstanding heritage railroad operated by the state of West Virginia. The commercial rail line closed in 1960, and state operations began in 1963. The park runs the largest fleet of geared locomotives in the world. The fleet includes not only Shays, but operational Heisler and Climax geared locomotives.

Strasburg Railroad / Norfolk & Western Railway No. 475 – The Strasburg Railroad began operation in 1837 and is the oldest continuously operating railroad in the United States. This locomotive is a star attraction at Strasburg. It is a 4-8-0 Mastodon M-class locomotive that was built by Baldwin Locomotive Works in 1906 and is now maintained in essentially perfect condition at the railroad. It is a former Norfolk & Western Railway steam locomotive that was part of Norfolk & Western's first order of M-class locomotives. No. 475 is the only known 4-8-0 operating in North America. The locomotive design is characterized by a somewhat cramped cab in which the fireman must actually stand on the tender to shovel coal because the firebox extends so far back through the cab. Strasburg excursions into the Pennsylvania Dutch Country began in 1959. The railroad is located across the street from the Railroad Museum of Pennsylvania.

New York Central & Hudson River Railroad No. 113—American Locomotive Company and General Electric Company built No. 113 as a joint effort in 1906 to operate on electrified tracks in and out of Grand Central Terminal in New York. It is a very early electric locomotive and is of the A+D+A class S-2 design. Electric locomotives became important in New York City very early on because of air pollution and safety issues associated with visibility on the tracks, especially in tunnels. The locomotive was renumbered to 3213 in 1908, 1113 in 1917, and then back to 113 in 1936. It was donated to the National Museum of Transportation by the New York Central Railroad in 1963. The locomotive is painted in New York Central dark gray, which is almost black.

⧊ Grand Canyon Railway No. 29—No. 29 is an SC-3 class 2-8-0 locomotive built in 1906 by American Locomotive Company. The engine operated on the Lake Superior & Ishpeming Railroad across Michigan's Upper Peninsula, very likely for both passenger and freight service. It has 50-inch drivers and weighs 185 tons. No. 29 was restored in 2004 at a cost of more than $1 million and twenty-six thousand hours of labor. The locomotive is in immaculate condition and can now operate on low-sulfur fuel oil or vegetable oil to transport passengers between Williams, Arizona, and the Grand Canyon South Rim. The Grand Canyon Railway has two steam engines but primarily operates vintage diesel engines on the run to and from the canyon every day. No. 29 can often be seen on display at the station in Williams.

➤➤ Clover Valley Railroad No. 8— No. 8 is a classic Virginia City/Mother Lode locomotive. The locomotive is sometimes known as Feather River Short Line No. 8. It is a 2-6-2, standard gauge locomotive built in 1907 by Baldwin Locomotive Works. It burns oil and is operational. The locomotive is based at the Gold Hill Depot in the Mother Lode region of Nevada and was originally Hobart Estates Company No. 8 and later the Hobart Southern No. 8. In 1938, Clover Valley Lumber bought the locomotive and kept it until it was sold to Feather River Railroad in 1956. It was subsequently donated to Feather River Short Line in 1958.

◄ ◄ **Philadelphia & Western No. 401 and Philadelphia Rapid Transit Company No. 8534**—Railway trolley and railed streetcars were an important adaptation of the locomotive for intracity passenger travel. Originally these cars and trains were pulled by horses and mules with some application of steam power (often called dummy locomotives) and cable systems. Railway trolleys began to electrify in the 1880s and 1890s, as soon as electrical service was available. Early models were wooden, but by the 1920s steel was used in their construction to provide a more stable ride with less maintenance. By the 1930s, thousands of miles of narrow and standard gauge trolley track crisscrossed America in every city of any size. The Great Depression and the introduction of buses led to a rapid demise of trolley and streetcar infrastructure in most cities. Saint Louis Car Company built No. 401 in 1907. It was not fully retired until the 1990s. No. 8534 is a steel trolley. It was built in 1926 by the J. G. Brill Company; No. 8534 was modernized in 1941 and phased out except for charters by 1957. Both of these units are now on exhibit in Scranton, Pennsylvania, at the Electric City Trolley Museum.

⋀ **(Left) Northwestern Pacific Railroad No. X112**—The Northwestern Pacific is a regional rail line that operates along the northern coast of California. No. 112 is the only surviving Northwestern Pacific steam locomotive; three sister locomotives were either wrecked or scrapped. American Locomotive Company built No. 112 in 1908 to burn oil. It has a 4-6-0 wheel arrangement. The locomotive is preserved in excellent condition and the beautiful colors of the Northwestern Pacific Railroad at the California State Railroad Museum. **(Right) Union Pacific**

Railroad No. 4466— Lima Locomotive Works built this 0-6-0 coal-burning locomotive in 1920. No. 4466 was the last shop switcher at the railroad's Cheyenne shops, and it then ended its Union Pacific career working at Grand Island, Nebraska, where it remained until 1973. In 1978 it was donated to the California State Railroad Museum. It was restored in 1984 and displayed. Although originally designed to burn coal, No. 4466 was converted to operate on oil, probably upon relocation to California. It was used in steam operations at the museum until 1999. (*Courtesy California State Parks*)

◄◄ **LaClede Christy Company No. 2**—
This 1907 0-4-0T switch engine was built by Davenport Locomotive Works for Laclede Christy Company for yard work. It is a 30-inch narrow gauge, coal-fired saddle tank engine. The locomotive was donated to the National Museum of Transportation in 1952. The engine cab is accessible for examination at the museum. The Laclede Christy Clay

Products Company is located in the Saint Louis area, where the company has operated a number of clay mines over the years. No. 2 was used to transport clay from the mines to the process works in Saint Louis, where the clay was used for making bricks, including fire bricks. The locomotive with a little train of clay wagons moving through Saint Louis was known locally as the *Dinky*.

⋀ **Southern Pacific Railroad No. 9**—
Southern Pacific Railroad No. 9 can be explored at the Laws Railroad Museum near Bishop, California in a beautiful setting on the quiet eastern side of the Sierra Nevadas south of Mono Lake and north of Death Valley. This is a narrow gauge oil burner that worked in the eastern Sierras region until it was retired. No. 9 was built

in 1909 by Baldwin Locomotive Works and features a 4-6-0 wheel configuration with 44-inch drivers. The locomotive remains in excellent condition and can be seen with an interesting lineup of railcars at the museum. Visitors are invited to ring the bell! The museum features a wonderful collection of historical machinery and other items.

◄◄ Lake Superior & Ishpeming Railroad No. 18—This beautiful locomotive was built in 1910 by the American Locomotive Company. It is a 2-8-0, oil-fired, standard gauge design that is now used on the La Veta Pass run east from Alamosa, Colorado, as part of the Rio Grande Scenic Railroad. The locomotive is a former Lake Superior & Ishpeming Railroad engine that was previously operated on the Grand Canyon Railway and the Mount Hood Railroad. The Lake Superior & Ishpeming Railroad is a short-line carrier located in the Upper Peninsula of Michigan. The railroad has been moving iron ore since about 1896. Today, the Lake Superior & Ishpeming is owned by Cliffs Natural Resources and operates over about 25 miles, from near Ishpeming east to Marquette.

► Calico and Odessa Railroad No. 5— At one time, Calico narrow gauge mining trains carried supplies and miners up to Barstow, California from down in Yermo, California, and also hauled ore from the mines. No. 5 is typical of the locomotives that may have been used. No. 5 is a 0-4-0ST built by C. W. Lovestead. This is a 30-inch-gauge locomotive that has been converted from steam to gasoline. It is operational. Today tourist trains circle through the hills providing an impressive overview of old mines and the valley below. No. 5 was photographed in Barstow. The manufacture date is unknown.

◄ ◄ **Freighters at Night**—The National Railroad Museum in Green Bay, Wisconsin includes a number of outstanding exhibits, but none is better than this lineup of three large, impressive locomotives facing the Fox River. **(Left) Lake Superior and Ishpeming Railroad No. 24**—This 2-8-0, coal-fired American Locomotive Company machine was built in 1910. **(Middle) Wisconsin Central Railway No. 2718**—This 4-6-2, coal-fired American Locomotive Company engine was built in 1923 in Schenectady, New York. No. 2719 was originally one of six Soo Line "Pacific" locomotives and was operated by Wisconsin Central Railway. It was donated to the National Railroad Museum in 1958, where it was used at the museum and for pulling excursions around the area. **(Right) Atchison, Topeka & Santa Fe Railway No. 5017**— No. 5017 is an oil-burning, 2-10-4 Baldwin Locomotive Works engine built in 1944 for the Atchison, Topeka & Santa Fe Railway. It spent most of its career in New Mexico, Oklahoma, and Colorado. This powerful locomotive was donated to the National Railroad Museum in 1959.

➤ **Panama Canal Railway Mule No. 662**— In 1914, General Electric supplied forty early electric locomotives, often called "lock mules" or just "mules," for the Panama Canal to guide ships through the narrow canal and locks. These very early electric locomotives operated on 220 volts at 25-cycles through a third underground rail. No. 662 and its sister units are five-foot gauge, rack/cog locomotives that operate on four flanged wheels located at the center of the engine. They are designed for operation at 5 miles per hour when not connected to a ship and 2 miles per hour for rack-and-pinion operation while towing. The mules operated in pairs on each side of the canal to keep ships centered as they passed through the three lock locations along the canal. The mules are equipped with a cab at each end and winch and cable systems for attaching to ships. No. 662 remained in service for fifty years and is now preserved at the National Transportation Museum in St. Louis.

➤ **Virginia & Truckee McCloud River Railroad No. 18**—McCloud River Railroad No. 18 is a Baldwin Locomotive Works 2-8-2 Mikado that was built in 1914 and is now operated on the Virginia & Truckee Railroad to lead excursions through the mountains between Carson City and Virginia City. The locomotive is in excellent cosmetic and operational condition. It fires oil, as do most other locomotives in the mountains and southwestern United States, where coal is not readily available. The run from Carson City up to Virginia City is over a steep grade. It passes through the historic and dramatic Mother Lode region, where trains once hauled in miners and hauled out ore.

➤➤ **Pennsylvania Railroad Nos. 3936 and 3937**—These class DD–1, 4-4-0 electric locomotives were developed in 1910–1911 to operate in the tunnels under the Hudson River and around the New York City and Long Island area. Visually they are huge and very striking and impressive machines. They were built at the Pennsylvania Railroad's Altoona Shops and relied on a third rail to draw DC power for operation. As electric locomotives, they, of course, did not emit the smoke characteristic of steam locomotives of the time and contributed to cleaner air in the metro area. In addition, they were considered safer underground for visibility reasons, following the tragic 1902 steam train collision in the Park Avenue Tunnel near Grand Central Terminal. The DD–1 consisted of essentially two 4-4-0 locomotives coupled back-to-back, and they were never operated separately. Thirty-three pairs were built, and they were capable of speeds to 85 miles per hour with their massive 72-inch drivers and side rods. Nos. 3936 and 3937 are the only remaining examples of this technology. They are preserved at the Railroad Museum of Pennsylvania.

Agricola de Guatemala No. 22—The South Park and Fairplay area of Colorado was the site of a gold rush beginning in 1859. The area, at an elevation of almost 10,000 feet, was connected to Denver in 1879 by the DSP&P over the famous Kenosha Pass. Locomotives became an important part of mining operations. No. 22, also known as No. 39, is a 2-6-0, H. K. Porter, oil-fired, 36-inch-gauge locomotive built in 1914. It is currently displayed in a beautiful mountainous scene at South Park City in Fairplay. As No. 39 the locomotive was used in Guatemala to transport bananas and other produce. Agricola de Guatemala was part of International Railways of Central America (IRCA), whose vision was to connect North and South America by rail.

Canadian National Railway No. 47—This locomotive was built in 1914 by Montreal Locomotive Works for the Grand Trunk Railway. When the Canadian National Railway was created in 1923, No. 47 became a Canadian National locomotive. This is a 4-6-4, coal-fired, tank locomotive with 63-inch drivers and a weight of about 275,000 pounds, which is large for a tank engine. It has a water capacity of 3,500 gallons. No. 47 was overhauled in 1958 and was in excellent condition when it was acquired by Steamtown National Historic Site. It was used for the first-ever Steamtown excursions in Scranton, Pennsylvania. However, the boiler certification was subsequently denied because maintenance records were lost in a roundhouse fire in Canada. Without the record, the boiler cannot be certified without an overhaul.

➤ Argentine Central Railway

No. 14—This locomotive reached the highest altitude ever achieved by a regular adhesion train (as opposed to a rack or cog railway) in the United States. It is an oil-fired Shay locomotive built by the Lima Locomotive Works in 1916 expressly for steep grades, sharp curves, heavy loads, and poor-quality track. To achieve the altitude record over a 6-percent grade, a geared locomotive such as No. 14 was required. The Argentine Central Railway Company operated in the mountains of Colorado from 1906 until 1918 to serve the silver mining operations of the region and the early tourist trade. The railroad lines ascended 13,587 feet up Mount McClellan. At the time, it was believed that Mount McClellan was 14,007 feet high, but this height was later disproved.

➤ ➤ Dresser Trap Rock Company

No. 1—Dresser Trap Rock is a stone and aggregate company that still operates in Wisconsin. No. 1, an interesting 0-4-0 locomotive, is part of the collection at the Iron Horse Central Railroad Museum. H. K. Porter built it in 1914. It is a small steam locomotive with drivers that are 36 inches in diameter. Between the 1860s and 1950, Porter produced more than eight thousand small locomotives, some of which are popular today as museum restoration projects because they are of a manageable size and design. Davenport, another producer of small locomotives, bought H. K. Porter in 1950.

◁ **Craig Mountain Lumber Company**
No. 3—No. 3 is a 1917, two-truck locomotive by Heisler Locomotive Works. The Heisler design featured two cylinders at 45-degree angles to form a V-twin arrangement. Power was transmitted through a driveshaft under the locomotive to propel the outboard axle on each powered truck through bevel gears in an enclosed differential or gear case on the axle between the truck frames. The inboard axle on each truck was then driven from the outboard one by external side connecting linkage. This design was well suited to logging, construction, and anything else needing torque and power. The Heislers were marketed as a faster alternative to the Shay design, the most popular geared locomotives. Also, with Heislers, the gearing was located inside the frame and more protected than with the Shays. Craig Mountain No. 3 can be seen on display at the Alamosa Station along the Rio Grande River in the San Luis Valley region of Colorado. This is a standard gauge engine, and it ran on oil.

◁ ◁ **Saint Louis–San Francisco Railway**
No. 1632—This impressive 2-10-0 Decapod was built by Baldwin Locomotive Works in 1918. It is a coal-fired locomotive from the legendary Frisco fleet. The ten drivers are each 52 inches in diameter. The locomotive was used primarily for branch work but also carried main-line passenger trains. No. 1632 is on prominent display at the Belton, Grandview, & Kansas City Railroad in Missouri. The Belton, Grandview & Kansas City Railroad is a heritage railroad and operates excursions on an old Frisco branch line. The railroad collection includes various locomotives, rolling stock, and other equipment.

➤ Canadian National Railway No. 5288—
This locomotive was intended for the Grand Trunk Railway, but because of the timing, it was actually delivered to the Canadian National Railway in 1919. Montreal Locomotive Works built it. It is a 4-6-2, coal-fired Pacific locomotive with 69-inch drivers for passenger service. No. 5288 is currently on static display at the Tennessee Valley Railroad Museum in Chattanooga.

➤ ➤ Pickering Lumber Company No. 2—
No. 2 is a 1918 three-truck Heisler locomotive with vertical, side-mounted cylinders and a driveshaft linked to the wheel sets. As with the Craig Mountain Lumber Company No. 3, this Heisler was designed and used for construction, logging, timber work, and other high-stress service. The Heisler design was in direct competition with the Shay locomotive design built by Lima; the Heisler was the fastest of the geared locomotives. With both Heisler and Shay locomotive designs, the tender rides on a pulling truck. Heisler built more than six hundred locomotives, but fewer than forty remain today. No. 2 was originally built for the Hetch Hetchy Railroad and was used in dam and aqueduct construction in California. This particular Heisler is a standard gauge, oil-fired engine that weighs in at about 150,000 pounds. No. 2 is a rare and historically significant locomotive. It is now owned and displayed by Travel Town Museum. Pickering Lumber was involved in an international controversy over the cutting of the mammoth sequoias from 1920 through the 1950s.

⚠ Milwaukee Road No. E-2 (Bi-Polar)—
In 1919, Chicago, Milwaukee, Saint Paul &
Pacific Railroad (Milwaukee Road) introduced
a series of five very impressive and distinctive
electric locomotives that came to symbolize
the railroad. Four of the five locomotives have
been scrapped. Only No. E-2 remains, and it
can be seen cosmetically restored to 1953
condition at the Museum of Transportation.
These locomotives were built by General
Electric for main-line service through the
Cascade Mountains. They were commonly

known as Bi-Polars because they used bipolar
electric motors. They could pull trains that had
previously required double-headed steam.
The Bi-Polars were massive in appearance,
with twelve gearless bipolar motors mounted
directly on the drive wheels for a 1B+D+D+B1
wheel arrangement. The hinged center section
contained a boiler to provide passenger heating.
They were rated at 3,200 horsepower (2,370
kilowatts) and could attain speeds of up to 70
miles per hour. The Bi-Polars were all rebuilt in
1953 but retired by the end of the decade.

◀ ◀ (Left) The *General II*—This is a former Red River & Gulf Railroad 4-4-0 steam locomotive built by Baldwin Locomotive Works in 1919. The engine was later purchased for use on the Louisiana Eastern Railroad in the 1950s and designated as No. 1. It is one of only four Louisiana Eastern steam engines still in existence. Following failure of this railroad, it was used to pull passenger tourist trains at Stone Mountain Park near Atlanta as Stone Mountain No. 104. It was known as the *General II*, after the General from the Great Locomotive Chase during the Civil War. In 1986, the locomotive was withdrawn from operation because of boiler and mechanical issues. In 2005, the engine was placed on a display outside the engine shed at the park and received a new coat of paint on the sides visible to passing trains. It was donated to the Southeastern Railway Museum in Duluth, Georgia in 2007 and was moved to the museum the following year, where it currently resides as the *General II*. **(Right) Chattahoochee Valley Railway No. 21**— Chattahoochee Valley Railway was a short-line railroad that operated between textile mills in Alabama and Georgia. Baldwin Locomotive Works built Chattahoochee No. 21 in 1924 for passenger service on the Tennessee, Alabama & Georgia Railway and was designated No. 201. Chattahoochee Valley bought the engine in 1935 for the short line and renumbered it to No. 21. The wheel arrangement is 2-8-0. It has 50-inch drivers, is a coal burner, and weighs 144,000 pounds. The locomotive is in cosmetically excellent condition and is on display at the Southeastern Railway Museum in Duluth, Georgia.

➤ Saint Louis–San Francisco Railway No. 4018—This locomotive, built by Lima Locomotive Works in 1919, has a very colorful history. It is a 2-8-2 Light Mikado machine designed to the United States Railroad Administration (USRA) specifications for World War I. This particular design evolved into the Berkshire locomotive over the next decade or two. No. 4018 is coal-fired, has 63-inch drivers, and weighs in at just over 300,000 pounds. It last operated in 1952 and was then donated to the city of Birmingham. The locomotive was cosmetically restored and displayed under cover for many years at the city's Kiddieland Amusement Park. In recent years, it has been moved to the historic Sloss Furnaces, where it has received additional cosmetic restoration.

◄◄ **Santa Maria Valley Railroad No. 1000 at Dusk**—American Locomotive Company built this locomotive in 1920. It uses a 2-8-2 Mikado wheel configuration, has 48-inch drivers, and weighs about 195,000 pounds. It was originally purchased by the city of San Francisco to provide freight and passenger service on the Hetch Hetchy Railroad east of San Francisco into the Sierra and Yosemite region. The engine was sold to the Newaukum Valley Railroad in Washington in 1924 but came back to California in 1944 when it was purchased by the Santa Maria Valley Railroad to service area oil refineries and to haul produce. Santa Maria donated the locomotive to Travel Town Museum in 1953.

▲ **(Left) Pennsylvania Railroad No. 3750**—Pennsylvania Railroad's class K4 Pacific 4-6-2 steam passenger locomotives are recognized by law as the "official locomotive" of the Commonwealth of Pennsylvania. No. 3750 is one of only two surviving examples of more than four hundred of these engines built between 1914 and 1928. No. 3750 dates to 1920. Pennsylvania Railroad built it in the railroad's shops at Altoona, Pennsylvania. The K4s were the premier reliable high-speed locomotives in the Pennsylvania Railroad fleet from soon after their introduction until the transition to diesel, a period of over three decades. No. 3750 is preserved by the Railroad Museum of Pennsylvania. **(Right) Pennsylvania Railroad No. 6755**—Dating to the 1850s, the railroad shops and facilities at Altoona, Pennsylvania were for many years the largest and most advanced in the world. The famous Juniata Shops were built at the site beginning in the late 1880s. Norfolk Southern still uses some of these facilities today. No. 6755 was built in the Altoona shops in 1930. It is a 195-ton, coal-burning, 4-8-2, Mountain-type locomotive with 72-inch drivers and a tender almost as large as the locomotive. The locomotive continued in heavy freight service until 1957. It is now on display at the Railroad Museum of Pennsylvania alongside No. 3750. No. 6755 is the lone survivor of the three hundred units built by the railroad, Baldwin Locomotive Works, and Lima Locomotive Works.

◀ ◀ **Abandoned Chassis**—The total steam locomotive production in the United States was approximately 175,000 engines over a period of about 125 years. Most were scrapped at the end of their useful lives, including many that were salvaged for materials during World War II. Only a few remain today, mostly in museums, on historic railroads, in private collections, at amusement and excursion demonstrations, or decaying out in the countryside somewhere.

Ⲗ **Mower Lumber Company No. 4**—This locomotive originally began service as Birch Valley Lumber Company No. 5 in 1922. It was renumbered to No. 4 when acquired by Mower Lumber in 1943, because the Mower fleet already had a locomotive No. 5. This is a very typical three-truck Lima class C-70 Shay locomotive built for logging in West Virginia during the 1920s. It features a diamond-shaped stack and has arch-shaped windows on the cab. It has 36-inch drivers and weighs about 160,000 pounds. This is a beautiful locomotive, and it is used in regular service at the Cass Scenic Railroad in West Virginia.

◄◄ **The Roundhouse at Railtown 1897**— The roundhouse at Railtown 1897 State Historic Park is one of only two fully functional short-line roundhouses in the United States. It was originally built as a steam locomotive service shop for the Sierra Railway and features a turntable that rotates to direct locomotives into stalls for service or storage. Each track and stall in the roundhouse is equipped with a service pit to allow workers to get under the locomotives for inspection, maintenance, and repair. A blacksmith shop and a machine shop are also part of the complex. Railtown 1897 State Historic Park is currently owned and operated by the California State Parks. It is used for historical preservation and educational and demonstration programs. In recent years, the roundhouse has been used to service, store,

and protect Sierra Railway Nos. 3, 28, and 34 locomotives. In 1929, the first movie was shot on the railroad property using railroad equipment at the site, providing an additional source of income for the railroad. Since that time, Railtown has been featured in a number of major motion pictures and television series. Items from the sets of *Back to the Future III*, *Petticoat Junction*, and other movies and television shows can be seen around the site. **(Far left) Sierra Railway No. 34**—This locomotive is preserved in the roundhouse at Railtown 1897 State Historic Park and is based on the 2-8-2 Mikado wheel configuration, which is larger than Sierra Railway No. 28, also preserved in the same roundhouse. Baldwin Locomotive Works built the locomotive in 1925. Sierra Railway used it in steam operations and later for excursions.

No. 34 last operated in 1979, but returning the locomotive to operational condition is under discussion. Although it is on display at Railtown, the locomotive has a private owner.
(Middle) Sierra Railway No. 28— Baldwin Locomotive Works built the No. 28 in 1922. The locomotive is part of the heritage collection at Railtown 1897 State Historic Park. For most of its life, No. 28 was used to haul lumber and rocks for dam construction projects, although it has done passenger and excursion service. This locomotive has a 2-8-0 wheel configuration and, like all steam locomotives at Railtown, is an oil burner. The locomotive can be seen in the roundhouse but currently is not in operational condition for safety reasons. Either No. 28 or its stable mate No. 34 will likely be brought to running condition in the not-too-distant future.

Ⱥ Rockport Railroad–Queens Subway Building Corporation No. 3—Today, Rockport, Maine is a picturesque New England coastal village along Penobscot Bay. But turn the clock back a century, and the waterfront is dominated by a huge lime plant complete with hot kilns, ovens, and shipping facilities. The Rockport Railroad connected the plant with a quarry a few miles away. The railroad dates to 1886. It operated two Vulcan Iron Works engines and thirty-five ore cars. No. 3 is a 1923 coal-fired Vulcan 0-4-0T locomotive that never actually worked in the quarry but is somewhat like the tank engines used there. It is now displayed in Rockport, adjacent to a historic lime kiln.

◀◀ **Grand Canyon Railway No. 4960**—
Baldwin Locomotive Works built this 2-8-2
Mikado locomotive in 1923 to post–World
War I United States Railroad Administration
standards. It operated as a freight and coal-
hauling engine for the Chicago, Burlington
& Quincy Railroad until the late 1950s. After
restoration, it began service on the Grand
Canyon Railway in 1996. Grand Canyon
Railway operates passenger service between
Williams, Arizona, and the South Rim of
the Grand Canyon. Until 1968, this line was
originally part of the Santa Fe Railway.

◀ **Driver Linkage**—The drive linkage
mechanism on a steam locomotive is
fascinating to watch in action. Most steam
locomotives have one piston, cylinder,
and linkage mechanism on each side of
the engine. The number and the sizes
of the drivers can vary, as can the size
of the cylinders. There is no gearing on
the traditional steam locomotive, so the
maximum speed and pulling torque are a
function of the driver diameter.

➤ **American Freedom Train No. 1**—This was the first of three steam locomotives to pull the 1975–1976 Freedom Train to commemorate the U.S. Bicentennial. An earlier diesel-powered freedom train had operated in 1947–1949 after World War II. No. 1 is a former Reading Lines 4-8-4 locomotive (No. 2101). Baldwin Locomotive Works built it in 1923 as a 2-8-0. It was later converted for faster, stronger operation in the Reading shops. The locomotive, which had been preserved since the steam era as a standby for Reading's Iron Horse Ramble excursions in the late 1950s and early 1960s, was repainted in red, white, and blue for the Freedom Train. The Freedom Train included ten display cars. It visited all forty-eight contiguous states, carrying treasures ranging from Washington's copy of the Constitution and the original Louisiana Purchase to Dorothy's dress from the *The Wizard of Oz* to Martin Luther King's pulpit to a rock from the moon. No. 1 is currently on static display at the B&O Railroad Museum.

➤ ➤ **Reading Lines No. 2124**—Baldwin Locomotive Works built No. 2124 in 1924 as a 2-8-0 Consolidation engine. In 1946 and 1947, the engine was rebuilt and converted to a 4-8-4 Northern configuration in the Reading shops, along with twenty-nine similar locomotives. These conversions were allowed at a time when construction of new steel locomotives was restricted because of World War II material shortages. These locomotives featured large surface area and Wootten fireboxes for burning anthracite coal. The rebuilt locomotives operated mostly in freight service until the mid-1950s and were then retired in favor of diesel equipment. From 1959 through 1961, No. 2124 was used to pull a Reading railfan excursion called the Iron Horse Ramble. In December 1959, the locomotive appeared in the opening scene of the film *From the Terrace* with Joanne Woodward. In 1963, the locomotive was retired and sold to Steamtown National Historic Site. Since that time, the locomotive has been declared restorable. In 1997, it was cosmetically restored and is now on static display at Steamtown.

◀◀ Scranton Roundhouse—The roundhouse at Steamtown National Historic Site dates to 1902. The roundhouse and the adjoining turntable are still fully operational for locomotive maintenance, storage, and restoration. Some areas are open to the public for walking tours. Steamtown is administered by the U.S. National Park Service.

⋀ Woodward Iron Company No. 38— No. 38 is a 2-8-0 Consolidation-type steam locomotive commonly used by American railroads for freight service between the 1880s and the 1920s. By the 1930s, the railroads needed larger and more powerful engines, and locomotives like No. 38 were relegated to branch line and switching work. Baldwin Locomotive Works built No. 38 in 1924 for short hauls and switching on the property of the Woodward Iron Company in Birmingham. During the early 1950s, it was sold to B&H Lumber Company and then donated to the Heart of Dixie Railroad Museum in the 1960s. It weighs in at 186,000 pounds and has 50-inch drivers. No. 38 is now a very popular attraction with train enthusiasts and photographers in Alabama. It can be seen on static display in excellent condition at the museum in Calera, Alabama.

Denver & Rio Grande Western Railroad Nos. 480, 481, 482, and 486—The Durango & Silverton Narrow Gauge Railroad is one of the most famous rail lines in the world. Its fleet of steam locomotives is maintained in immaculate condition, and the tracks through the San Juan Mountains are absolutely spectacular. It uses two classes of locomotives designated as K-28 and K-36. Nos. 480, 481, 482, and 486 are K-36 locomotives, the larger class, indicating traction or track adhesion of about

36,000 pounds force. Five sister locomotives from the 480 series are owned and operated by Cumbres & Toltec Scenic Railroad, located east of Durango, Colorado along the Colorado–New Mexico border. Baldwin Locomotive Works built all these locomotives in 1925 as narrow gauge, coal-fired, 2-8-2, Mikado-type locomotives for the Denver & Rio Grande Western Railroad. The following images from the Durango & Silverton Narrow Gauge Railroad are included in this portfolio:

⋏ Rio Grande No. 480—This 1925 coal-fired, Mikado locomotive was built by Baldwin for the Denver & Rio Grande Western Railroad and was purchased by the Durango & Silverton in 1971. It is one of four K-36 locomotives operated by the railroad to provide excursion service through the San Juan Mountains.

➢ ➢ On the Rio Grande Highline—The Animas Canyon Highline between Durango and Silverton is one of the most spectacular scenes in all of mountain railroading. This famous rock cut was built in 1881 and 1882. The track rests on a shelf blasted into the cliff face 400 feet above the river. Drillers swung from ropes suspended over the cliff to drill and plant the black-powder charges.

◁ ◁ **Durango & Silverton Nos. 480 and 486**—In 1925, Baldwin built a series of 10 K-36 Mikados for freight service across the Denver & Rio Grande Western system. In this image, No. 480, with freight cars, waits on a siding, while No. 486 steams by in the glorious fall morning air.

⋏ **Durango Roundhouse**—The original Durango Roundhouse was built in 1881 and modified several times over the years. In 1989, fire destroyed most of the building. It was rebuilt the next year using the original brick design where possible. A museum and exhibit areas are part of the roundhouse.

◀ ◀ **Durango & Silverton No. 482**—
Durango & Silverton maintains a fleet of
steam locomotives in immaculate condition.
No. 482 is a K-36, indicating tractive power of
about 36,000 pounds.

⋏ **Hot Ashes**—During dumping of an ash
pan, the fire can either be banked on the
grate for the next run or extinguished if the
locomotive will not be used again for some
time. Here, the fire will be banked for a quick
start-up the next the morning.

⋀ Denver & Rio Grande Western No. 486—Powering along a grade of about 2 percent at about 5 or 10 miles per hour with mixed freight in tow, No. 486 displays an impressive column of smoke and steam. The locomotive requires about 6 tons of coal and 10,000 gallons of water per day. No. 486 was retired in 1962 and displayed at the Royal Gorge from 1967 until 1999, when it became operational again for service on the Durango & Silverton.

➢ ➢ Climbing through the San Luis Mountains—The picturesque San Luis Mountains provide a dramatic backdrop for Durango & Silverton No. 480 and a lineup of classic boxcars. This 1925 locomotive operates on 44-inch drivers with an empty weight of 187,100 pounds.

Cumbres & Toltec Scenic Railroad Nos. 483, 484, 487, 488, and 489—The Cumbres Pass and the Toltec Gorge provide a dramatic setting for scenic excursion railroading in southern Colorado and northern New Mexico. This stretch of track was once part of the Denver & Rio Grande Western Railroad and is now featured on the Cumbres & Toltec Scenic Railroad. The railroad operates a fleet of steam locomotives, including five 2-8-2 Mikado locomotives built by Baldwin Locomotive Works in 1925 as part of a series of ten locomotives. These locomotives, numbered 483, 484, 487, 488, and 489, are often referred to as K-36 class and are sisters to the K-36 locomotives at Durango & Silverton Narrow Gauge Railroad. The *K* designates the Mikado wheel arrangement, and the 36 is for the measure of traction in thousands of pounds force. These were the last new narrow gauge locomotives built for the Denver & Rio Grande Western Railroad. They were followed in 1928 by the C-41 class, in which the *C* stands for Consolidation or 2-8-0, and the 41 again represents the tractive force in thousands of pounds. The following images from the Cumbres & Toltec Scenic Railroad are included in this portfolio:

A Cumbres & Toltec No. 489 at Los Pinos Water Tank—No. 489 is shown in the expansive Horseshoe Curve adjacent to the 1890 Los Pinos Valley water tank. Water is supplied through a pipeline from a well and reservoir about a half a mile away above the valley floor. The Horseshoe Curve allows the locomotive to climb through the valley at a very low ascent grade on the way to Antonito, Colorado.

➤➤ Cumbres & Toltec No. 484—In a classic scene, No. 484 steams into Chama, New Mexico, alongside the 1924 coal tipple, the only surviving wooden coal tipple in the United States and one of the few operational coal tipples in the world. The small building in front of the tipple is used to store and dry traction sand, which is essential for the Cumbres & Toltec locomotives on the 4 percent grades leading to Cumbres Pass.

Cumbres & Toltec No. 488—In a scene that has changed little since the 1880s, No. 488 runs along the southern Rockies near the border between New Mexico and Colorado on its way to the 10,015-foot Cumbres Pass, the highest point in U.S. steam railroading. The wooden structure in this image is the base of a former water tank that was used in filming several movies, including *Indiana Jones and the Last Crusade*.

The Antonito Station—Dating to the early 1880s, Antonito is a very interesting railroad company town in southern Colorado. Narrow gauge tracks run southwest into New Mexico and standard gauge lines extend north to Alamosa. The Cumbres & Toltec station is very conventional in design, with waiting areas, ticketing booths, and crew quarters. The yard includes a shop for servicing railcars and locomotives, a large water tank, several display locomotives, and assorted rolling stock.

◄ ◄ **Chama Shops**—Chama station was established in 1881 as a midpoint service depot between Alamosa and Durango and near the difficult Cumbres Pass, where helper engines were needed. Some of the shop structures date as far back as 1889, with a full complement of classic and modern tools and maintenance supplies for servicing locomotives and rolling stock. A modern shop was constructed in the late 1970s with a massive lift for raising locomotives off their drivers.

⋀ **Taking on Water**—The impressive water tank at the edge of the Chama yard is said to be the only double-spouted water tank still being used in the United States.

➤ **Southern Railway No. 1401**—This locomotive is a feature display in the National Museum of American History. It was built by the American Locomotive Company in 1926 as a Pacific-type engine with a 4-6-2 wheel arrangement. No. 1401 was used to pull Southern's top class of passenger trains, especially through the Carolinas, until it was retired in 1952. It has 73-inch drivers and weighs in at just over 300,000 pounds. It could pull twelve to fifteen steel passenger cars with a top speed of 80 miles per hour and travel 150 miles between water stops. The locomotive is in beautiful green, gold, and silver cosmetic condition and is also considered to be mechanically operational. This locomotive is famous for pulling President Franklin D. Roosevelt's funeral train in 1945.

➤ ➤ **Motorized Railcars (Speeders)**— The earliest speeders date to the 1890s. They became common railroad equipment in the early twentieth century. These vehicles were called speeders because they were much faster than the older hand-cranked and hand-pumped vehicles they replaced. Later models were capable of speeds up to 30 or 35 miles per hour with a small gasoline engine providing the motive power. They often had a windshield and a top and could tow a trailer. After about a century of use, they were retired and replaced by special flanged-wheel trucks and SUVs in the 1980s and 1990s. Many speeders remain, and they are collected and restored by individuals and clubs across North America.

◀ ◀ **E. J. Lavino and Company No. 3**—
This 1927 American Locomotive Company
coal-fired steam locomotive was operated by
E. J. Lavino Steel Company in Pennsylvania.
No. 3 is a 0-6-0 saddle tank–type locomotive
(often designated with a *T* following the
wheel arrangement: 0-6-0T) with 44-inch
drivers. It was first owned by Poland Spring
Company in Maine. It came to Lavino in 1949
to be used as a switch engine in a manganese
blast furnace facility. It uses Stephenson valve

gear and has a wheelbase of just over 10 feet.
In 1966 it was donated to F. Nelson Blount and
subsequently Steamtown National Historic
Site. It is preserved in the roundhouse at
Steamtown, in beautiful restoration condition.
Saddle tank locomotives are well suited to
switching work at a plant site where carrying
large quantities of water and coal is not
necessary. The absence of a tender makes the
locomotive very compact, mobile, and easy to
handle for yard work.

▲ **Republic Steel No. 294**—This
locomotive sat for many years in a railroad
graveyard—one of many similar places
across the country. Fortunately, No. 294 has
since been fully restored cosmetically and
is on prominent display at Lynnville Railroad
Museum in Lynnville, Tennessee. No. 294 is
a 2-6-2 engine. Baldwin Locomotive Works
built it in 1927. It began its career in East
Saint Louis, then worked in Cleveland, Ohio,
and in Birmingham.

◄ **Chesapeake & Ohio No. 490**—In 1926, the American Locomotive Company constructed No. 490 for the Chesapeake & Ohio Railway (C&O). It was built as a 4-6-2 Pacific locomotive for passenger service and worked on several famous eastern lines, including Washington, D.C. routes. Just after World War II, C&O wanted to upgrade its passenger service and compete with other streamlined, art deco designs. In 1946 and 1947, No. 490 and several similar Pacifics were converted to 4-6-4 Hudsons and shrouded with streamlining in classic Chessie yellow and stainless steel. Matching sets of streamlined passenger cars were also produced. Although never used for the glamorous routes envisioned by C&O, the No. 490 is indeed a striking and impressive locomotive. Today, the locomotive can be seen indoors at the B&O Railroad Museum. It weighs in at almost 390,000 pounds and has 74-inch drivers.

➤ ➤ **Southern Railway No. 610 / Texas & Pacific Railway No. 610**—This is a large, fast, and powerful 2-10-4 engine built by Lima Locomotive Works for Texas & Pacific Railway in 1927. It was designed for fast freight service. No. 610 was operated by Southern Railway for excursions in the late 1970s under a lease arrangement with a foundation in Texas. It is now on display at the Texas State Railroad Museum in Palestine, Texas. This locomotive should not be confused with Tennessee Valley Railroad No. 610. Commercial steam operation at Southern Railway ended in 1953, but the company operated a popular excursion program from the mid-1960s until the early 1990s, through the merger with Norfolk & Western Railway in 1982. Some excursions have resumed recently.

Chicago & Illinois Midland Railway No. 551—This is the only surviving Chicago & Illinois Midland (formerly Chicago & Midland) steam locomotive. The locomotive is a 2-8-2 light Mikado built to World War I (USRA) standards. It is a standard gauge, coal-fired engine. Thousands of Mikados were built. During World War II, an attempt was made to change the name from Mikado to MacArthur, but the Mikado name generally remains in use. Chicago & Illinois Midland Railway operated primarily to transport Illinois Basin coal to power plants in the state of Illinois. When the Clean Air Act passed in 1970, the railroad began to move Powder River Basin subbituminous coal from Wyoming instead because of the lower sulfur content of the fuel from that region.

Denver & Rio Grande Western Railroad No. 495—This 2-8-2, coal-fired, narrow gauge locomotive was built in the Denver & Rio Grande Western Railroad Burnham Shops in 1928. It is part of the railroad's K-37 class and was one of a group of locomotives popularly known as Sports Models. Ten of these locomotives were rebuilt by converting 2-8-0 standard gauge Baldwin equipment to narrow gauge. No. 495 was sold to the Cumbres & Toltec Scenic Railroad in 1970. It is currently in picturesque display condition in the yard at Antonito, Colorado, adjacent to the Cumbres & Toltec station.

CHAPTER 3

THE GREAT DEPRESSION AND THE WAR YEARS
(1930–1949)

After a steady climb in number of passengers and tons of freight for almost a century, the 1930s and 1940s saw harder times for the railroads and the locomotive manufacturers. The Great Depression and World War II, along with automobiles, trucks, and airplanes, and improvements to roads and airfields, reduced the demand for trains and rail travel. Trains had lost much of their former glamor, and the automobile was so convenient.

By the end of World War II, electric and diesel technologies had been around for several decades. Diesel-electric locomotives were now fully commercial, and their value relative to steam began to be realized. Steam locomotives were still cheaper to purchase, and steam infrastructure was in place all across the continent, but diesels were more economical to maintain, required less maintenance, needed fewer repairs, and provided a smoother ride. They could also be operated in series by a single crew to provide whatever serial power might be needed. The era of steam was coming to an end.

At the same time, this era saw the production of the largest, most advanced, and most magnificent steam locomotives in history. They had art deco styling, articulated chassis, and multiple sets of cylinders and pistons. These steam locomotives could singlehandedly haul almost 40,000,000 pounds of freight.

Statistically speaking, the total American steam locomotive production in just over one hundred years was about 175,000 units. According to the U.S. Department of the Interior, of that total about 1,950 steam locomotives remain today. Around 250 of these are more-or-less operational, but only about one hundred can actually run as of 2014.

➢ ➢ **Flagg Coal Company No. 75**—This 1930, coal-fired, saddle-tank locomotive is a 0-4-0ST switcher engine built by Vulcan Iron Works in Pennsylvania for quarry operations. In 1991 it was purchased by private owners, who restored it to excellent condition over the next decade. No. 75 is small enough for shipment on a large eighteen-wheeler truck. It is currently used for train rides, excursions, and educational demonstrations across the United States. The locomotive never actually operated as Flagg Coal Company No. 75 during its working career.

The Calera Station—The locomotive helped define the growth of the United States, from the location of cities to the delivery of the mail, passengers, and goods. Even the smallest towns had stations. The classic, beautiful designs of these stations became sources of community pride. At one point, there were more than 120,000 active railroad stations across the country, including the old Wilton Station, now known as the Calera Station.

(Left) Rio Grande Southern Railroad Galloping Goose No. 2—Galloping Goose No. 2 was built in Ridgway, Colorado, in 1931 from a Buick Master Six sedan. Its job was to carry a small amount of freight, mail and express, and up to four passengers travelling between Durango and Ridgway and remote destinations across southwest Colorado. The intent was to replace steam locomotives with more economical equipment. No. 2 was the second of seven unique and innovative rail vehicles conceived and produced by Rio Grande Southern as the railroad operated on the edge of bankruptcy through the Great Depression and World War II. In 1939, No. 2 was rebuilt with a 1926 Pierce-Arrow car body and a more powerful Buick engine. It was painted silver in 1935. This vehicle is still operational and is preserved by the Colorado Railroad Museum. **(Right) Rio Grande Southern Railroad Galloping Goose No. 6**— In 1934, Goose No. 6 was built from the body of a Buick sedan and a Buick engine. Like the other Galloping Geese, No. 6 was designed to run on two trucks, with the rear one powered. Most of the parts used to build No. 6 came from Goose No. 1, which at that time had been recently scrapped. No. 6 weighs about 8,700 pounds and is about 25 feet 8 inches long. This goose replaced steam-powered freight and work trains on the Rio Grande Southern, but it never saw regular passenger service. Later, No. 6 was rebuilt with Pierce-Arrow body and engine. Today it is preserved at the Colorado Railroad Museum. It is still operational.

◅ ◅ **Rio Grande Southern Railroad Galloping Goose No. 5**—Goose No. 5 was built in 1933 by Rio Grande Southern Railroad at a very low cost from a Pierce-Arrow body and a 1936 Pierce-Arrow engine. In 1946, this Goose was rebuilt with a Wayne Bus body and a World War II surplus 361–cubic inch GMC engine. No. 5 weighs in at about 14,770 pounds and is about 43 feet 3 inches long. When No. 5 became operational, Rio Grande Southern discontinued use of its last steam locomotive. After the railroad closed in 1951, No. 5 and the other Geese were transitioned to excursion service. They were each officially named Galloping Goose by the Rio Grande Southern (the name had been used unofficially for years). Their livery was modified to list the tourist landmarks of the line, and a goose drawing was also painted on each side. Goose No. 5 was bought by the city of Dolores, Colorado, to be displayed at the preserved Rio Grande Southern Depot in Dolores. It was completely rebuilt in 1998 by the Galloping Goose Historical Society in Dolores and is now operational again. It runs regularly on the Cumbres & Toltec and the Durango & Silverton railroads.

◅ **Pennsylvania Railroad/Conrail No. 4800**—Baldwin Locomotive Works and General Electric built this locomotive in 1934. It is an articulated prototype GG-1 design. The immense locomotive weighs in at 475,000 pounds and uses overhead AC with dual pantographs. No. 4800 was capable of speeds up to 100 miles per hour with a power output of 4,620 horsepower (3,450 kilowatts), and it set a speed record of 102 miles per hour in 1935. The design features twelve traction motors and six drive axles. The locomotive was used initially for passenger service and later for freight hauling before retiring in 1979. Known as *Old Rivets*, No. 4800 was added to the North America Railway Hall of Fame and designated a Historic Mechanical Engineering Landmark in 1983. During a long career, it served under Pennsylvania Railroad, Penn Central, and Conrail systems. It is currently on display at the Railroad Museum of Pennsylvania, where it received cosmetic restoration in the early 1980s.

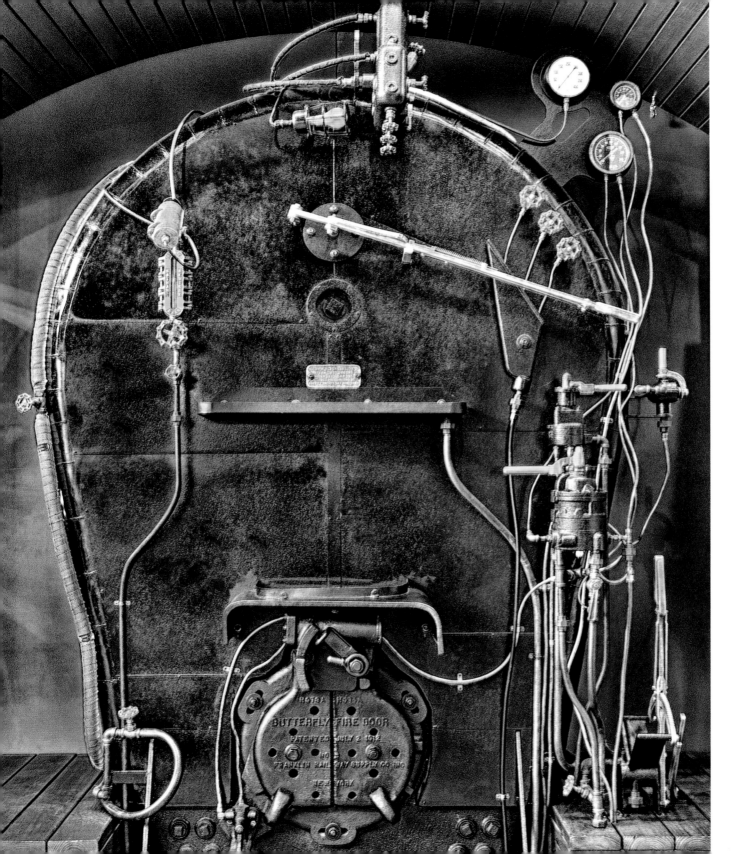

◄ **Firebox, Boiler, Levers, and Valves**—
The locomotive cab is the control
compartment for a steam locomotive.
This is the area where the engineer and
the fireman operate the locomotive. It
is generally located at the back of the
locomotive, at the rear of the firebox and
boiler. The tender where the fuel and
water are carried is usually just behind the
cab area. The firebox door can be seen
near the bottom center of the image. The
throttle and brake levers and other controls
and gauges are located to the right. This
particular demonstration cab is located at
Steamtown National Historic Site.

➢ ➢ **Burlington Route *Pioneer
Zephyr***—The Burlington Route "Silver
Streak" *Pioneer Zephyr* began operation
in 1934. This train was built by the Budd
Company for the Chicago, Burlington &
Quincy Railroad and features extensive
use of stainless steel and a relatively early
and remarkably successful diesel-powered
locomotive. The train set was designed to
be permanently articulated together and
required new technology in stainless steel
welding. In May 1934, the *Pioneer Zephyr*
set an average speed record of 77 miles
per hour for travel between Chicago and
Denver. On one section of track, it was
clocked at 112 miles per hour, approaching
the land record at the time of 115 miles
per hour. The *Pioneer Zephyr* was the
first of many diesel-powered, streamlined
passenger trains. Other Zephyrs soon
followed; the trains were fast and popular.
Other diesel locomotive designs were
not very common in the United States
before the 1950s, especially for high-speed
passenger service. The *Pioneer Zephyr* is
now on prominent display at the Museum
of Science and Industry in Chicago. This
locomotive was the inspiration for *Silver
Streak*, a very popular movie in the 1930s.

◀ ◀ **Southern Railway No. 2839**—No. 2839 is a streamlined, coal-fired Canadian Pacific Royal Hudson 4-6-4 that is now part of the exquisite Nethercutt Collection in Los Angeles. This locomotive originally served in the elegant, streamlined steam locomotive fleet of the Canadian Pacific Railway. Montreal Locomotive Works built it in 1937. No. 2839 was later leased, painted in Southern Railway livery, and operated by Southern for excursions, but it was generally considered underpowered. It was sold to a group in Pennsylvania in the 1980s. Subsequently, the locomotive was acquired by the cofounder of the Merle Norman cosmetics corporation and is now part of Merle Norman's transportation museum, where it has been restored for display.

Ʌ *Dwight D. Eisenhower*—*The Dwight D. Eisenhower* is a British-built steam locomotive. It was formerly known as the London & North Eastern Railway (LNER) No. 60008. It served as General Eisenhower's tactical command center during World War II and was later shipped with several cars to the National Railroad Museum in Green Bay for restoration and preservation. This 4-6-2 steam locomotive was built by LNER Doncaster Works in Britain in 1937 and is in excellent condition. Historically, this is a very significant piece of American heritage. The Eisenhower locomotive was loaned to the National Railroad Museum in York, United Kingdom, for a three-year period beginning in late 2012. At the museum in York, the locomotive has undergone additional restoration and a slightly revised and more historically accurate paint scheme.

➤ **Chicago, Burlington and Quincy Railroad No. 9908 (*General Pershing Zephyr*)**—This locomotive, also known as the "Silver Charger" (after General Pershing's horse), was built in 1939 and was the last of the streamlined, stainless Budd Company Zephyrs. It was powered by a General Motors 1,000-horsepower, V-12 diesel engine linked to an electric generator. This was the only locomotive in this Zephyr series that was not articulated; each car was separate and coupled for better handling and customizing of train length. It was used extensively on a fast run between Kansas City and St. Louis but also served on many other routes during World War II. Most of the stainless steel train sets retired soon after the war, but this locomotive continued in service until 1966. Following retirement, No. 9908 was given to the National Transportation Museum in St. Louis, where it remains on display today.

◁ General Motors FT Demonstrator No. 103—This 1939 locomotive was the first General Motors FT unit produced, and it is now designated as a National Historic Engineering Landmark. The FT is the locomotive that first made the railroads think seriously about diesel-electrics to pull freight trains. Like Fairbanks-Morse, General Motors used existing submarine technology for motive power in the early F units. No. 103 and the other original FTs used a 1,350-horsepower (1,010-kilowatt) drive system, but they were semi-permanently coupled with a matching B unit, which doubled the power. This invaluable locomotive is preserved at the National Museum of Transportation.

➢ ➢ Oliver Iron Mining Company No. 900—This locomotive is an excellent example of a very early diesel-electric switch engine from American Locomotive Company. It was manufactured in 1940. Designated as an Alco HH1000, the locomotive was powered by a turbocharged, inline, six-cylinder diesel engine that produced 1,000 horsepower at a rating of 750 kilowatts. The locomotive was used in Minnesota's iron ore industry. It was donated to the Lake Superior Railroad Museum in 1973 and is still in general working order.

◄ Pennsylvania Railroad No. 4890—
No. 4890 is a GG1 locomotive, one of the most successful and strikingly styled locomotives in history. GG1s appear in more ads and movie clips than any other locomotive in history. Robert Loewy did not do all the styling, but he contributed to the unique and now-familiar appearance of the machine. General Electric and Pennsylvania Railroad built a total of 139 GG1s between 1934 and 1943 at the Altoona Shops. No. 4890 was built in 1940. These locomotives were used exclusively in the Northeast Corridor, where overhead electrical service was available. At 79 feet 6 inches and 475,000 pounds, they were huge, very dependable, and capable of speeds up to 100 miles per hour. Despite their length and weight, GG1s were built with essentially a ball-and-socket joint at the middle and could flex to make tight turns and curves. A mechanical linkage called a pantograph was fitted above each end of the locomotive for connection to overhead electrical service. Twelve 385-horsepower (4,620-kilowatt total) GEA-627-A1 traction motors drove the GG1's 57-inch driving wheels on six axles. GG1s last operated in 1983, although there were earlier attempts to retire them. GGIs were used to pull the funeral trains for both President Franklin D. Roosevelt and Senator Robert F. Kennedy. No. 4890 was repainted in classic Tuscan Red in 2000 and is displayed in showroom condition at the National Railroad Museum.

⋀ Union Pacific Railroad No. 4012—
No. 4012, along with No. 4017 described below, is one of twenty-five Big Boy locomotives built by American Locomotive Company between 1941 and 1944 for Union Pacific. They are among the largest locomotives ever built. A single Big Boy could pull a 7,000,000-pound train over the 1.14-percent grade of the Wasatch Range unassisted. No. 4012 was built in 1941 and retired in 1962. It ran for more than one million miles during that time, carrying freight between Cheyenne, Wyoming and Ogden, Utah. With four cylinders and a 4-8-8-4 articulated wheel arrangement, Big Boys were over 85 feet long (almost 133 feet with the tender) and weighed in at 762,000 pounds. They operated on coal, including subbituminous western coal, and could achieve speeds of 60 miles per hour with high reliability and safety. These locomotives competed with Baldwin's 2-8-8-4 Yellowstones, which were considered more powerful but were slower. No. 4012 is one of eight remaining Big Boys. It is displayed at Steamtown National Historic Site. This is a locomotive that could be restored to working order; the main concerns, other than cost, would be substantial tracks and lines to support the weight of the machine in operation. Union Pacific has announced the restoration of No. 4014, a project that is expected to take three to five years.

◀◀ Duluth, Missabe & Iron Range Railway No. 225—The huge Yellowstone 2-8-8-4 locomotive No. 225 is one of the largest locomotives in the world. Of the eighteen Yellowstones built, this is one of three remaining examples. It has generally been described as among the finest and most powerful engines ever to operate on a railroad anywhere. A Yellowstone still holds the record for the heaviest U.S. train ever at over 19,000 tons (38,000,000 pounds). Baldwin built the Yellowstones between 1941 and 1944 to pull long, heavy loads of iron ore in the northern Iron Range region of Minnesota during World War II. They were also used on the Rio Grande. A Yellowstone could burn 10 to 12 tons of coal an hour and evaporate water into steam at an amazing rate of 12,000 gallons per hour. Yellowstone No. 225 is on display along a highway in Proctor, Minnesota.

◀ C&O No. 1604—Along with the American Locomotive Company Big Boy and the Baldwin Locomotive Works Yellowstone, the Lima Locomotive Works Allegheny was one of the world's largest and most powerful locomotives. These 2-6-6-6, articulated four-cylinder locomotives weighed about 780,000 pounds and could produce 7,500 peak horsepower. Sixty of these behemoths were built to haul heavy coal trains through the Allegheny Mountains and to occasionally pull passenger trains at 60 miles per hour. No. 1604 is one of two remaining Allegheny locomotives. It can be seen in excellent cosmetic condition at the B&O Railroad Museum.

➤ Union Pacific Railroad No. 4017—
No. 4017 is one of the eight Union Pacific Big Boy locomotives built by American Locomotive Company that survive today. No. 4017 was built in 1942 and retired in 1961. Like all the Big Boys, it ran for just over one million miles during its career, pulling heavy loads over steep grades through the Rockies and Sierras. The Big Boy tender, called a Centipede, is amazing in itself. It has fourteen wheels and a capacity of 56,000 pounds of coal and 25,000 gallons of water. A Big Boy consumed coal at a rate of 12 tons per hour. No. 4017 is displayed indoors in excellent cosmetic condition at the National Railroad Museum, where visitors can climb into the cab and visit with Santa during the holidays.

➤ ➤ Norfolk & Western Railway No. 1218—The spectacular Norfolk & Western 1218 is the only surviving four-cylinder, articulated, 2-6-6-4 class A locomotive in the world. It was built in 1943 at the Norfolk & Western Roanoke Shops as a fast freight locomotive. It could carry 60,000 pounds of coal and 22,000 gallons of water. The drivers are 70 inches in diameter. The class A locomotives were a little smaller than the Union Pacific Challengers but achieved a better overall performance record. In its later years of its operation, No. 1218 was the most powerful steam locomotive in existence and was capable of speeds of more than 70 miles per hour. It was retired from regular rail service in 1959, was used for a time as an industrial boiler, and later operated in excursion service until 1992. Today, the locomotive is owned by the O. Winston Link Museum and is on display at the Virginia Museum of Transportation. Restoration of No. 1218 is a topic of constant discussion.

> **Arriving in the Mist**—Amazingly, clocks and timetables were not standardized across the United States when the locomotive and the railroad arrived. With the interconnection of railroads and multiple locomotives sharing the same tracks and running around the clock in all kinds of weather, timing and schedules had to be worked out for safety reasons. The official clock in many towns came to be hung in the railroad station. In 1883, the American Railway Association implemented the four standard U.S. time zones, a key communication development for the entire continent.

Southern Railway No. 2716—No. 2716, a 2-8-4 Berkshire locomotive, was actually C&O No. 2716 and part of the railroad's K-4 Kanawhas class of engines. But the locomotive became more famous by leading excursions, especially during a lease to Southern Railway in the early 1980s. Southern Railway never actually owned or operated Berkshires during the steam era but detailed the engine to look as it might have looked if it had been a Southern locomotive from the 1940s. Regardless of the livery, this is a classically beautiful engine with a colorful history. It was outshopped in 1944 by American Locomotive Company, has 69-inch drivers, and weighs 460,000 pounds. While on lease in the 1980s, an inexperienced fireman damaged the firebox, and the engine was never been brought back to dependable, operational condition. Attempts to weld cracks in the firebox failed, and a new firebox sleeve is needed to resolve the problem. No. 2716 is preserved as a static display at the Kentucky Railway Museum. The Berkshires have become famous in recent years as the locomotive featured in the *Polar Express* movie!

◀◀ **Alabama By-Products No. 4046**— No. 4046 is a 0-6-0, coal-fired locomotive that was built to wartime specifications in 1944 by Lima Locomotive Works for the U.S. Army. The locomotive was subsequently purchased and used until 1962 by the ABC Coke Plant near Birmingham, Alabama. In 1969, the locomotive was donated to the Heart of Dixie Railroad Museum. It has been restored cosmetically for prominent display at the museum under cover and out of the weather.

ʌ **(Left) Erie Mining Company No. 4211**—This F9A locomotive was purchased and used as a mine ore hauling engine throughout its career. It was built by the General Motors Electro-Motive Division in 1956. LTV Mining Company donated the locomotive to the Lake Superior Railroad Museum in 2002. **(Right) Duluth, South Shore & Atlantic Railway No. 101**—This

1945 American Locomotive Company RS-1 has been restored to operational condition but is currently stored at the Lake Superior Railroad Museum, where it may receive additional restoration attention. The four-axle, RS-1 was rated at 1,000 horsepower (746 kilowatts) with electrical components by General Electric. No. 101 is owned by the Soo Line Historical and Technical Society.

◀ ◀ **Pennsylvania Railroad No. 5901—** This Electro-Motive Division E7 locomotive, along with its scrapped sister, No. 5900, were the first two diesel locomotives delivered to Pennsylvania Railroad. They demonstrated clearly to management the reliability of diesel relative to steam motive power. They were built at General Motor's plant in LaGrange, Illinois in 1945. No. 5901 operated reliably until retirement in 1973.

The locomotive is powered by two EMD 12-cylinder, 1,000-horsepower diesel engines and two 600-volt DC generators. The EMD E series of locomotives feature the distinctive and still popular bulldog nose that was a cosmetic characteristic of EMD locomotives until about 1970. This beautifully restored locomotive in Tuscan Red is one of the most significant displays at the Railroad Museum of Pennsylvania.

⋏ **Delaware, Lackawanna & Western Railroad No. 664—**Lackawanna No. 664 is a 1,500-horsepower Electro-Motive Division F3A diesel-electric unit ordered by Bangor & Aroostook Railroad (B&A) of Maine in 1948. The F3 was a very beautiful and popular series of locomotive. They were built to haul heavy freight and were powered by a Winton 16-cylinder engine with four traction motors, one on each axle. They were rated

at a top speed of about 65 miles per hour. Originally enumerated as B&A No. 46, the locomotive was sold to the Anthracite Railroads Historical Society in 1986 and painted in Central of New Jersey colors. It came to Steamtown National Historic Site in 2009, where it underwent complete restoration and was painted in Lackawanna freight colors and numbered 664. No. 664 has a sister A unit numbered 663.

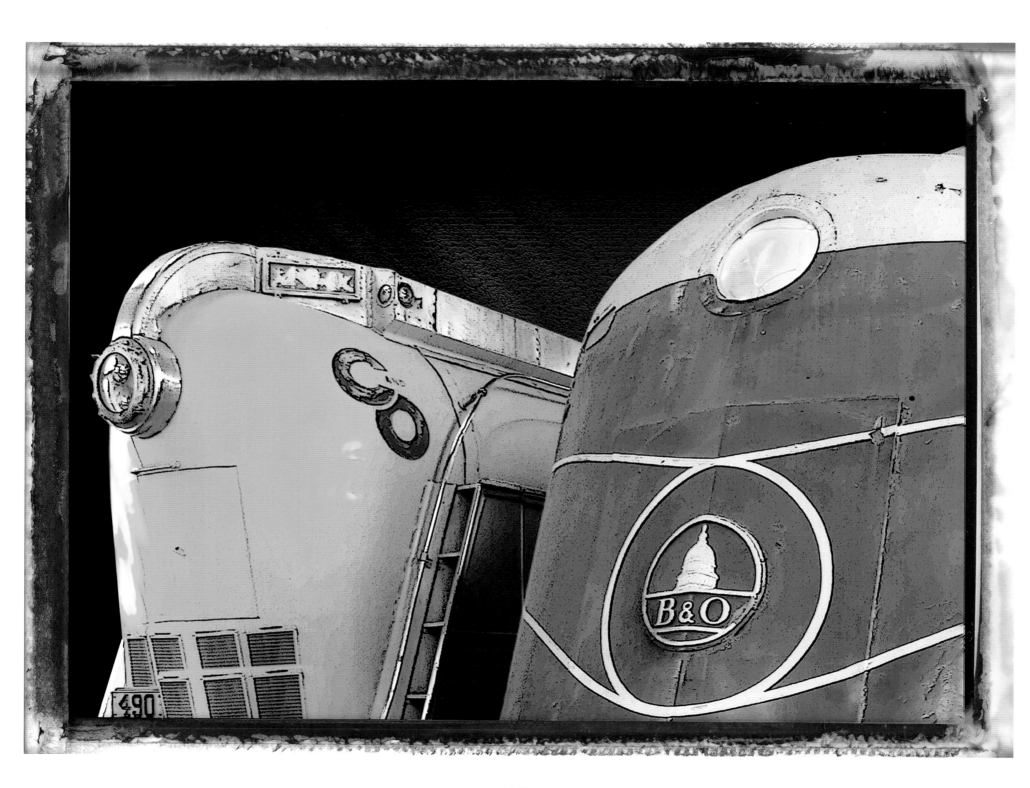

◀ ◀ **Streamliners**—Faced with growing competition from automobiles and airplanes, streamlining was an attempt by the railroads to attract passengers back to their trains, especially after the Great Depression. Streamlined styling made locomotives look new, fast, and more exciting. Streamlining was added to old, existing locomotives to save money, and it was also ordered for new models. Of all the thousands of steam locomotives produced in the United States, fewer than about 250 were streamlined, in part because of the timing and the transition to diesel.

➤ **Light Rays**—Brilliant light rays streaming from the western sky appear to give this old steam locomotive new life. The low camera angle, the depth of the scene, and the beautiful subtle color and energy of the light transform a somewhat ordinary scene to a dramatic statement.

CHAPTER 4

THE ERA OF DIESELIZATION (1950–1960)

In the mid-twentieth century, as today, there was a great love for the iconic steam locomotive. But as we all know, these magnificent machines were displaced across America by diesel-electric engines for passenger and freight service and road and switching operations.

It was not the transition from steam to diesel that surprised the locomotive manufacturers. Rather, it was the pace of the changeover. The traditional steam locomotive manufacturers envisioned a slow replacement over several decades while they developed diesel-electric technology and new production facilities. But the change came swiftly. It was essentially complete in about a ten-year period.

The General Motors Electro-Motive Division emerged as the clear winner and dominant producer, a position it would hold until the 1980s. In distant second was a partnership between the American Locomotive Company and General Electric. General Electric had actually led in the development of the first viable diesel-electric locomotive back in the mid-1920s, but its early production and sales lagged behind those of General Motors.

The timing of World War II helped assure that the Electro-Motive Division, and ultimately General Electric, would prevail over Baldwin Locomotive Works and American Locomotive Company. While EMD and GE continued to develop the diesel locomotive during the war, Baldwin and American were charged with producing older steam designs for the war effort. By the end of the war and the early 1950s, EMD and GE were far ahead in diesel design and technology development. All the major railroads had switched to diesel by 1960, and Baldwin, the world's largest locomotive manufacturer, ceased production in 1956.

➤ ➤ **A Century of Railroading**—Early twentieth-century and early twenty-first-century locomotives stand alongside each other in this image as if poised for a race. Although dieselization was complete shortly after the mid-twentieth century, there remains a great love for the iconic steam locomotive.

➤ Norfolk & Western Railroad No. 611—
Norfolk & Western's famous No. 611 streamlined J-class 4-8-4 locomotive was one of the last of thirteen J-class locomotives built entirely by Norfolk & Western. This is one of the most popular and recognizable engines in the country. No. 611 has been in the railroading news in recent years because it is being restored to running condition. This engine was built in 1950 at the East End Shops in Roanoke, Virginia, with streamlined shrouding. It was capable of speeds up to 110 miles per hour. No. 611 is certainly an impressive and powerful coal-fired locomotive. It was used by Norfolk & Western on its most important passenger trains. In later life, it derailed twice during excursion runs with passengers aboard, but no one was killed. In recent years, it has been on display near the shops where it was built at the Virginia Museum of Transportation. The cost of building the No. 611 in 1950 was about $250,000. In the early 1980s, it was rebuilt in Birmingham at Southern Railway's Norris Yards. Plans are afoot to use the locomotive for excursions in the fall of 2014.

◁ ▷ **Southern Railway and Norfolk Southern Railway Excursions**—At the close of the steam era, major railroads preserved a few of their classic locomotives for possible future promotional, railfan, and employee excursion programs. One of the most successful of these programs was at Southern Railway. In 1966, Southern Railway launched a full-scale steam excursion program using restored locomotive Southern Railway No. 4501. When Southern merged with Norfolk & Western in 1982, the excursion program continued. Several locomotives were used over the years, including Southern Railway Nos. 610 and 2716, Norfolk & Western Nos. 611 and 1218, and Nickel Plate No. 765. After two accidents, the program was discontinued in 1994. In 2010, the program was restarted with Southern Railway No. 630.

Saint Elizabeths Hospital No. 4—This 1950 engine was the last steam locomotive manufactured by H. K. Porter and one of the last made in the United States. It is a 0-4-0T (tank) locomotive that was used to pull coal hopper cars from a B&O Railroad site to the Saint Elizabeths Hospital in Washington, D.C. It was affectionately known as *Little Lizzie*. The locomotive was later transferred to the U.S. Army, then sold to Cass Scenic Railroad, and most recently given to the B&O Railroad Museum in 1980.

Northwestern Pacific Railroad Fairmont MT-14 Railway Motorcar (Speeder)—Fairmont Gas Engine and Railway Motor Car Company in Fairmont, Minnesota, was the largest and most popular manufacturer of motorized maintenance vehicles in North America. At one time, it offered nineteen different models. The MT-14 was a common model series. Several thousand were made beginning as early as the 1920s, with most dating to the period between the mid-1930s and the mid-1950s. This particular Fairmont is painted in colorful Northwest Pacific livery.

Baltimore & Annapolis Railroad No. 50—The brightly colored Baltimore & Annapolis Railroad No. 50 was purchased from General Electric in 1950 and provided freight service until 1986, when it was retired and donated to the B&O Railroad Museum. No. 50 is a GE "70 Tonner" switcher/industrial diesel-electric locomotive with a 600-horsepower, Cooper Bessemer 6-cylinder engine. It was the railroad's only freight locomotive for many years. The Baltimore & Annapolis railroad can be traced to 1887 and provided passenger, commuter, and freight service in central Maryland between Baltimore and Annapolis. The passenger line was electrified in 1906 and was ultimately replaced with bus service in 1950. Much of the line is now part of the Baltimore light rail system.

⋀ **Reading Lines No. 903 and 902**—These General Motors Electro-Motive Division diesel-electrics were two of the first six FP7s ordered by Reading in 1950 to replace steam locomotives in passenger service. They subsequently passed to Southeastern Pennsylvania Transit Authority (SEPTA) and Conrail and were retired in 1981. Restoration of the locomotives was completed in 1995,

and they are now on display in fine-looking condition at Steamtown National Historic Site. The FP7s were designed for passenger service and are equipped with steam generators. They are 1,500-horsepower units with a 16-cylinder diesel engine and four General Motors traction motors for travel at a maximum speed of 65 miles per hour. These two locomotives are used to pull railfan excursions.

➢ ➢ **Lookout Mountain Incline Railway No. 2**—The Lookout Mountain Incline Railway in Chattanooga dates back to 1895. At a 72.7-percent grade, it is one of the steepest passenger railways in the world. It is about 1 mile in length through the historic Saint Elmo neighborhood. Railway car No. 2 has been retired and is on exhibit at the Tennessee Valley Railroad Museum. The manufacture date is unknown.

**➤ Verde Canyon Railroad No. 1510 and
No. 2164**—No. 1510 and its mate, No. 1512,
are General Motors Electro-Motive Division
diesel-electric FP7 locomotives built in the
early 1950s. For the purists, these locomotives
were essentially extended versions of the
extremely popular F7A locomotives. About
380 were produced. They were used for both
passenger and freight service. Nos. 1510 and
1512 were built for operation in Alaska and
were later purchased from Alaska Railroad and
refurbished by Verde Canyon Railroad. Alaska,
where starting a steam locomotive in the cold
climate was often difficult, was the perfect
market for early diesels. These locomotives
are currently two of only about a dozen
remaining FP7s in North America, with others
sold and serving internationally. No. 2164 was
built by the Electro-Motive Division for the
Atchison, Topeka & Santa Fe Railroad in 1950.
No. 2154 is an updated GP7, known as the
GP7u. The locomotive is powered by a V-16,
1,500-horsepower (1120-kilowatt) powertrain.

➤ ➤ Verde Canyon Trestle—The Verde
Canyon Railroad operates excursion runs out
of Clarkdale, Arizona, over a dramatic canyon
line that was built in the early 1900s to move
ore from the Jerome mines. Much of the
rugged canyon region is accessible only by
the railroad, which includes several interesting
trestles and a tunnel.

◁ ◁ **Jersey Central Lines No. 1554**—This Central Railroad of New Jersey RS-3 diesel-electric locomotive was built in 1953 by American Locomotive Company. Technically, it is powered by a 1,600-horsepower, V-12 turbocharged, 4-stroke diesel engine, 1,200-kilowatt generator, and four GE traction motors. The RS-3s used a B-B wheel arrangement. American Locomotive Company and Montreal Locomotive Works produced almost 1,400 of these distinctive engines between 1950 and 1956. No. 1554 has been immaculately rebuilt and is used in excursion service across eastern Pennsylvania and New Jersey. Central Railroad of New Jersey is a historically significant Class I railroad that operated across New Jersey and into Pennsylvania for more than a century beginning in the 1830s. Many are most familiar with the railroad's station, Communipaw Terminal, on the Jersey shore of the Hudson River near the Statue of Liberty.

⋀ **Western Pacific Railroad No. 917**—No. 917 is a 1,500-horsepower General Motors Electro-Motive Division 16-cylinder supercharged 567 diesel-electric locomotive. It was capable of speeds up to 65 miles per hour. It was delivered to Western Pacific in 1950 as part an A-B-B-A set of F7 locomotives, costing the railroad about $650,000. No. 917 was originally lettered No. 917-D. It was used to help retire many of the railroad's steam engines from freight service. While serving on the Stockton to San Jose auto trains, the A-B-B-A set became one of the most popular and photographed locomotives of the time. After the Western Pacific merger with Union Pacific and as part of a trade with the Bay Area Electric Railroad Association, No. 917 came to the Western Pacific Railroad Museum (Feather River Rail Society) in Portola, California in 2005. The Western Pacific Railroad Museum is located at a former Western Pacific locomotive facility, adjacent to the Union Pacific main line through the Feather River Canyon.

⋀ **Western Pacific Railroad Nos. 805A and 925C**—These locomotives date to 1950, and No. 805A was used to head the prestigious California Zephyr. No. 805A is a General Motors Electro-Motive Division FP7 A locomotive. It is powered by a V-16 diesel engine to produce 1,500 horsepower (1,100 kilowatts). In later life, the locomotive was used for shorter-line and freight work. No. 925C is an F9Bu that was built by General Motors Canada to produce 1,750 horsepower (1,200 kilowatts). This locomotive did not actually operate on the Western Pacific but was purchased and cosmetically outfitted to match No. 805A to recreate a classic A-B set. Both are operational and are maintained by the Western Pacific Railroad Museum.

⋏ Diesels at Portola—The Western Pacific Railroad Museum maintains one of the largest collections of historic diesel locomotives in North America. The primary mission of the museum is to preserve the history of the Western Pacific Railroad.

⋀ Chicago, Burlington & Quincy Railroad No. 9939A—This striking locomotive was used to lead the Burlington Lines Zephyr on the famous run between Chicago and Denver. It is a 1950 General Motors Electro-Motive Division E8 locomotive. The E8s were powered by a pair of V-12 supercharged diesel engines rated at a total of 2,275 horsepower (1,678 kilowatts). Each engine drove its own generator, which in turn provided power to one of the two sets of traction motor trucks. They were capable of speeds to 85 miles per hour. No. 9939 was rebuilt in 1973, retired in 1992, and is now preserved in display condition at the National Museum of Transportation. Several other E8s are preserved around the United States, and some are fully operational.

➤➤ Tennessee Valley Railroad No. 610— No. 610 was built in 1952 by Baldwin-Lima-Hamilton Corporation for the U.S. Army. This 2-8-0 Consolidation-type locomotive has been a very popular and familiar sight across the Tennessee Valley around the Chattanooga area, where it provided service at the Tennessee Valley Railroad Museum for a number of years. The locomotive also appeared on several Norfolk Southern steam excursions during the early 1990s. No. 610 was one of the last steam locomotives built in the United States and is currently undergoing restoration at the museum. The Tennessee Valley Railroad Museum is the largest operating historic railroad in the South, and it runs passenger trains every day from spring until fall on a route through the eastern part of the city. It also runs special excursions. A highlight of the railroad's daily local passenger runs is a trip through the old 1858 Missionary Ridge tunnel and over four bridges.

➤ Missionary Ridge Tunnel—In 1856, East Tennessee & Georgia Railroad began work on the Whiteside Tunnel, known as Missionary Ridge Tunnel, in Chattanooga, Tennessee. Geographically, this ridge had prevented railroad development across a fairly large area beyond the mountains and along the Tennessee River. In recent decades, the tunnel has been restored and maintained by the Tennessee Valley Railroad Museum.

➤ ➤ Reading Lines No. 467—No. 467 is a 1952 American Locomotive Company RS-3 locomotive powered by an Alco 244, 12-cylinder, four-stroke, turbocharged diesel engine that drives four GE 752 traction motors. The engine is 55 feet long, weighs about 229,000 pounds, and had a top speed of 65 miles per hour. This was a very versatile locomotive. Almost 1,500 of the locomotives were produced between about 1950 and 1956, and a number are still in existence, working on short lines, tourist lines, and hauling freight. No. 467 can be seen at Steamtown National Historic Site in Reading Lines livery. This is a beautifully styled engine.

➤ East Chattanooga Station—This station is part of a working railroad yard for the Tennessee Valley Railroad Museum. It includes an 80-foot turntable and complete locomotive maintenance and restoration shops. The station forms one end of the line used for daily excursions.

⋀ Canadian National Railway No. 902 with Snowplow—Canadian National No. 902 was built in 1952 by the Electro-Motive Division, which at the time was part of General Motors. This locomotive joined the fleet just three years after Newfoundland became a province in 1949 and the rail system, which was all narrow gauge, became part of Canadian National Railway. No. 902 is a relatively early narrow gauge diesel-electric. Nine of these models, known as the NF110, were built. No. 902 is preserved at the Lewisporte Train Park in Newfoundland, with a snowplow that would have been essential to rail operation in Newfoundland. There have been no operating rail lines on the island of Newfoundland since 1988.

Alabama Power Company No. 40—The No. 40 is an imposing Davenport steam-only, fireless locomotive built in 1953. It has no boiler and can operate for about four hours on a steam charge from a power plant or other steam supply. At Plant Barry steam-electric plant, it was known as the "thermos bottle." Davenport produced locomotives from 1902 until 1956, and this is one of the finest remaining examples of its equipment. This locomotive can be seen at the Heart of Dixie Railroad Museum.

Rio Grande No. 5771 and 5762—This awesome locomotive set in yellow livery was used to lead the Rio Grande Zephyr when it operated between Denver and Salt Lake City from 1970 until 1983. The Denver–Salt Lake City run was the last non-Amtrak passenger train to operate in the United States. When the Rio Grande Zephyr was discontinued in 1983, these locomotives were used for one season in 1984 to lead ski trains from Denver on the weekends, and then they were retired. Nos. 5771 and 5762 are Electro-Motive Division F9s, which are 1,750-horsepower (1,300-kilowatt) diesel-electric locomotives produced between February 1953 and May 1960 by General Motors Electro-Motive Division. The F9 was the fifth model in GM-EMD's highly successful F series of diesel locomotives. These locomotives were obviously operated as an A and a B unit set. The Rio Grande owned a total of four each, A and B units. No. 5571 was rebuilt after a fairly serious wreck in Utah. Both locomotives were donated to the Colorado Railroad Museum in 1996, and the exhibit at the museum today is outstanding.

Canadian National Railway No. 906—Canadian National No. 906 is on display at the beautiful stone Newfoundland Railway Station in St. John's, which is now known as the Railway Coastal Museum. No. 906 was the only NF110 built in 1953 by Electro-Motive Division and was part of the consist that pulled the last passenger train across Newfoundland in 1969. This locomotive with a C-C wheel arrangement weighs in at just over 100 tons, features a 1,200-horsepower (890-kilowatt) diesel-electric drive system, and could reach speeds of up to 60 miles per hour on the 3-foot 6-inch narrow gauge track across the province. The first locomotives and railway operations in Newfoundland date to 1881. The Newfoundland Railway tracks were characterized by steep grades and sharp curves with snow and ice issues throughout the winter. At 906 miles, the Newfoundland Railway was the longest narrow gauge line in North America. When Newfoundland and Labrador became a Canadian province in 1949, the rail line became part of Canadian National Railway and underwent an extensive and costly upgrade. The last trains on the island of Newfoundland ran in 1988. Several examples of locomotives and rolling stock are preserved across Newfoundland, but most rails have been removed.

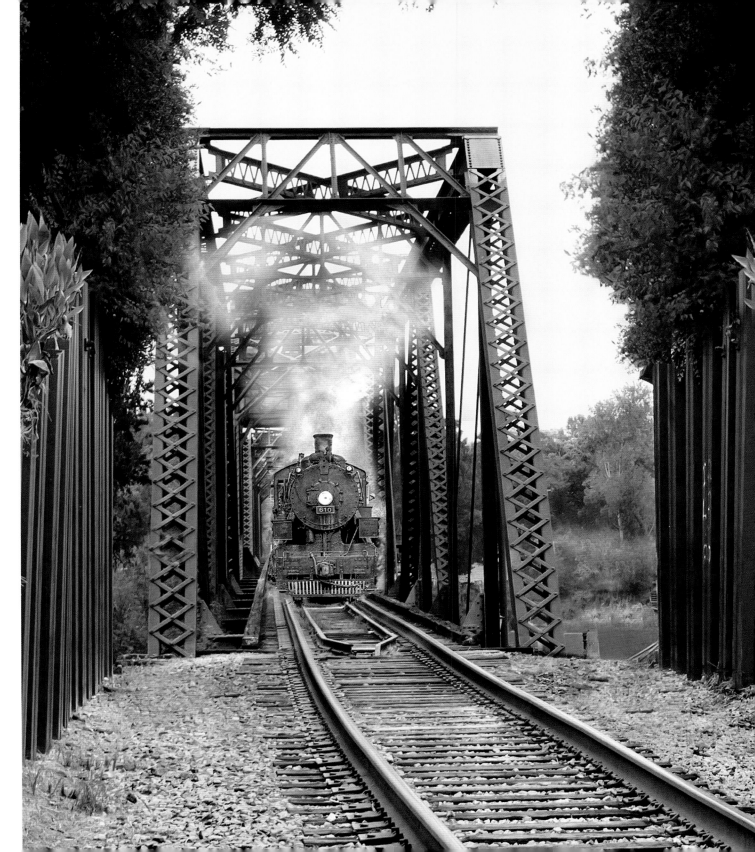

◁ ◁ **U.S. Army No. 1861**—No. 1861 is a Model HIZ-44 Fairbanks-Morse and Company diesel-electric switch engine that was built in 1953 for the U.S. Army Depot in Anniston, Alabama. The Army donated the locomotive directly to the Heart of Dixie Railroad Museum in the 1980s, and it has since been sold to a group in Texas—although the Heart of Dixie retains two other similar Fairbanks-Morse locomotives. Fairbanks-Morse diesel engines were unique in that they used an opposed-piston design that was developed for use in submarines during World War II. After the war, the engine was simply adapted for locomotives and a number of designs were offered. Fairbanks-Morse locomotives were never particularly popular. The company exited the U.S. market in 1958 and the Mexico market about five years later, but continued to operate in Canada through the 1960s.

➤ **Truss Bridge Crossing**—Truss bridge design and construction were fundamental to the development of railroads in America, especially in the East, which had many hills and streams. In 1856, the first railroad bridge was completed across the Mississippi River at Rock Island, Illinois, using truss construction. Iron truss bridges became common in the United States beginning in about 1870. Most truss bridges before that time, including the original Rock Island Bridge, were constructed of wood, which was vulnerable to fire and rotting.

⋀ Rock Island Railroad No. 2 (The Aerotrain)—The Aerotrain was a streamlined train set introduced by General Motors Electro-Motive Division Styling Section in the mid-1950s to try and win back passenger business that was being lost to the airlines, buses, and automobiles. No. 2 and No. 3 were built as commercial test models along with matching passenger cars based on GM buses. The Aerotrain was capable of speeds up to about 106 miles per hour and was economical on fuel because it was lightweight. The styling was certainly eye-catching, and many riders gave the trains a try at New York Central, Pennsylvania Railroad, Union Pacific, and Santa Fe. The riders and the railroads were not impressed. The Aerotrain proved to be underpowered, was difficult to service, and offered a rough, cramped ride, more like a bus from that era. Both train sets were quickly assigned to commuter service at Rock Island and were retired by 1966, about a decade after introduction. The No. 2 train can be seen and examined at the National Railroad Museum, and the Rock Island No. 3 Aerotrain is on display at the Museum of Transportation.

⋀ Canadian National Railway No. 932— No. 932 is an Electro-Motive Division diesel-electric locomotive built for Canadian National's narrow gauge rail system in Newfoundland. No. 932 dates to 1956 and is one of 38 units, known as the NF210, built before 1960. Along with Canadian National No. 931, No. 932 was involved in a derailment near Gander, Newfoundland in 1984. The locomotive is preserved at the old station in Bonavista, Newfoundland on a branch line where lighter locomotives typically operated. Passenger rail service ended across Newfoundland in 1969. Bonavista is the location where John Cabot landed in 1497 and claimed North America for England.

CHAPTER 5

THE MODERN ERA (1960–PRESENT)

The locomotive market in North America today is dominated by two principal diesel-electric locomotive manufacturers, General Electric Transportation Systems and Caterpillar's Progress Rail Services Electro-Motive Diesel (formerly the Electro-Motive Division of General Motors). In the first decade of the twenty-first century, they combined to produce more than ten thousand new locomotives, mostly rated at 4,000 horsepower or more.

Decades of competition between these two companies has led to a very refined, efficient, and reliable product. Typical specifications include refined turbocharging, 16- to 20-cylinder engines, six-axle designs with enhanced traction, alternating current technologies, electronic controls, refined cooling, and low environmental emissions. During the 1980s, General Electric became the number one producer of locomotives in the world. It now holds about 70 percent of the U.S. market.

Today, both locomotive manufacturers and the Class I railroad operators are major growth industries, and both are very profitable. For the railroads, economic growth in recent decades came as a result of more balanced and less oppressive regulation and improved operations. Freight shipping rates have decreased, and volumes are up. Railroad mergers have also improved performance. More than one hundred Class I railroads have become less than ten major railroads today. The largest are Union Pacific, BNSF, CSX, Norfolk Southern, Canadian National, Canadian Pacific, Kansas City Southern Railway, and Amtrak.

The locomotives and railroads of the twenty-first century are perceived as safer, more efficient, and more environmentally friendly than trucks and highway transport. Looking forward, expect more economical locomotive operation, lower emissions, hybrid fuel engines including liquefied natural gas, enhanced computer applications, satellite tracking and spotting systems, faster stopping brakes with recovery of braking energy, and possible remote control. This is our American railroading heritage in an exciting and promising new era for the locomotive.

➤➤ **Savannah & Atlanta Railway No. 2715**—This General Motors Electro-Motive Division GP-35 was built in 1964 and is the only surviving diesel from the Savannah & Atlanta Railway fleet. The *GP* stands for "general purpose," and it is a second-generation design with added power and improved mechanical performance. This locomotive features a 16-cylinder, turbocharged diesel engine with 2,500 horsepower (1,860 kilowatts). More than 1,300 of these locomotives were built, and a number of similar locomotives remain in service across the country. No. 2715 can be seen at the Georgia State Railroad Museum in Savannah, Georgia. Savannah & Atlanta Railway was incorporated in 1915 and operated in east-central Georgia with headquarters in Savannah. The railroad was purchased by the Central of Georgia Railway in 1951 and subsequently merged into Southern Railway in 1963. No. 2715 is painted in the classic black, gold, and white colors of Southern Railway.

◀◀ **Burlington Northern Santa Fe (BNSF) Railway No. 1559**—This Electro-Motive Division SD38P was built in 1966 as Southern Railway No. 3099. It is built on an SD35 frame. *SD* stands for "super duty" or "special duty," and it features six axles for additional traction and heavy hauling. No. 1559 is a 16-cylinder, 2,000-horsepower (1,500-kilowatt) locomotive.

This series of locomotives was ruggedly built for long service, and many of these machines are still in use today. This particular locomotive operates frequently out of the East Thomas Yard in the Arkadelphia area of Birmingham, but in recent years it has been photographed in many locations across the Southeast and Midwest.

⋀ **Pioneer & Western Railroad No. 3**—Over the last few decades, the market for steam locomotives, at least new steam locomotives, has been amusement parks and educational centers. Pioneer & Western Railroad No. 3 is a good example of a large amusement park locomotive. It is a 4-4-0 locomotive that was built in 1967 by Crown Metal Products in Pennsylvania. Crown produced more than fifty beautifully and classically styled steam

locomotives, primarily for amusement parks, between about 1960 and the late 1980s, before going out of business in the 1990s. No. 3 is one of Crown's largest locomotives, a 36-inch, narrow gauge design, that can be seen in a remarkable display on the turntable at the historic Huntsville Railroad Depot in Alabama. The locomotive was built for Pioneer & Western Railroad in Fort Lauderdale, Florida, along with a set of closed coaches and a caboose.

⋀ Wisconsin Central Railroad No. 7495—
This 1967 General Motors Electro-Motive
Division SD45 diesel-electric locomotive
was originally Northern Pacific No. 3617. It
is a six-axle, 20-cylinder, 3,600-horsepower
(2,680-kilowatt) machine. A total of 1,260

SD45s were built. Some of the early models
were noted for reliability issues, especially
with the crankshafts. Most or all have now
been retired. No. 7495 can be seen in very
good condition at the Lake Superior
Railroad Museum.

⋀ The Bessemer Station, Norfolk Southern Railway No. 8466—The Alabama Great Southern Railroad Station at Bessemer, Alabama, was designed and built by railroad employees in 1916. Because of the culture at that time in the South, there were separate passenger waiting rooms and complete facilities for white men, African Americans, and white women. No. 8466 is a General Electric C40-8W that was built in 1994 and is rated at 4,000 horsepower (3,000 kilowatts). It is part of the GE Dash-8 Series.

➤ **Union Pacific Railroad No. 6944**—
No. 6944 is an amazing Electro-Motive Division DD40AX diesel-electric locomotive built in 1971. The DD40AX has the distinction of being the most powerful diesel locomotive ever built at 6,600 horsepower (4,920 kilowatts). At 98 feet, it is also the longest diesel locomotive in history. Despite the massive size of these machines, they could attain speeds of up to 80 miles per hour. Although this particular locomotive was not manufactured until 1971, these locomotives are collectively known as Centennials in commemoration of the centennial of the 1869 First Transcontinental Railroad completion. A total of forty-seven Centennials were built between 1969 and 1971, and they were essentially the equivalent of two locomotives connected together to produce a dual engine design from existing Electro-Motive Division components. A number of Centennials remain, and No. 6944 in all its massive scale can be inspected at the National Museum of Transportation.

➤ ➤ **Union Pacific Railroad Nos. 2175, 2236, 2184, and 2232**—The SD60 was a very successful and trouble-free locomotive for the Electro-Motive Division. Union Pacific purchased eighty-five of the 1,140 units produced, and all but one are still in service in 2014. These four Union Pacific locomotives date to 1986–1988 and were designed for heavy-duty and medium-speed service. The SD60 is a six-axle, 16-cylinder, 3,800-horsepower (2,800-kilowatt) locomotive. This four-unit lash-up was photographed high in the Sierra Nevada Mountains near the California-Nevada border. No. 2236 displays the slogan *We Will Deliver* from the company's 1990s mission statement.

Amtrak No. 82—The Capitol Limited operates daily between Washington, D.C. and Chicago. The train is typically powered by a pair of GE P42DC locomotives. In this 2011 image, it is led by No. 82. The P42DC, which was first produced in 1997, has a top speed of about 110 miles per hour. The Capitol Limited route passes through some of the most historic and scenic regions of the United States, including the amazing 885-foot Maryland Heights B&O tunnel (built in 1898) and bridgework at Harpers Ferry, West Virginia. Harpers Ferry gained fame during the Civil War because of its strategic importance. It lies where the Potomac and Shenandoah rivers converge and where the Appalachian Mountains and the B&O Railroad and the Chesapeake & Ohio Canal came together.

⋏ CSX No. 29—No. 29 is a General Electric AC44CW diesel-electric locomotive with a powerful 4,400-horsepower (3,300-kilowatt) drivetrain. As the GE designation indicates, this engine uses AC traction motors and also includes the optional self-steering truck design to reduce wheel and rail wear. This locomotive dates to the early 1990s. Production of this model ended in 2004 because the diesel engine design could not meet the 2005 EPA Tier II emission requirements. These engines have proven to be very formidable freight haulers and are often seen leading coal unit trains. The *CW* indicates a C truck design (three axles) with a W or wide cab. The locomotive is seen emerging from the 900-foot 1908 Brock's Gap Tunnel through Shades Mountain in Alabama.

◄ ◄ **BNSF No. 6821**—No. 6821 is a General Electric ES44C4 locomotive with AC traction motors and a rating of 4,400 horsepower. This locomotive is from the new Evolution series of engines designed to meet tough EPA Tier II emission requirements. No. 6821 was built in 2011 and uses a four-stroke V12 engine to produce 4,400 horsepower (3,280 kilowatts). This locomotive has two fewer powered axles with supposedly no loss in pulling power. BNSF ordered sixty of these engines. This scene is adjacent to the old Route 66 in western Arizona.

⋏ **CSX Crossing**—Along with a tunnel and a high trestle, crossing tracks and trains are among the most exciting settings in railroading. On busy main lines, it is often possible to time the crossing for two trains!

⋏ **(Left) Norfolk Southern Railway No. 2562**—This classic Electro-Motive Division SD70 diesel-electric locomotive has been in service since 1998. No. 2562 is powered by a 4,000-horsepower (3,000 kilowatts), V-16 engine and is equipped with DC traction motors. This engine was assembled from a kit at the Juniata Shops in Pennsylvania and originally operated as a Conrail locomotive ordered to Norfolk Southern specifications. **(Right) Norfolk Southern Railway No. 7643**—No. 7643 is a General Electric Evolution series ES40DC locomotive powered by a 4,000-horsepower, V-12 engine and DC traction motors. These locomotives are distinctive because of their large, winglike radiator structures that extend out from the hood. The wings are necessary for additional cooling to make this 2007 locomotive meet the 2005 Tier II EPA emission standards. The Evolution series of locomotives has been named by *Trains* magazine as one of the "Ten Locomotives that Changed Railroading."

⋀ BNSF at West Bottoms—In the late nineteenth century, the West Bottoms area of Kansas City, Missouri was a major center of rail activity, and it is still the oldest warehouse and industrial district in the city. Today, this is a wonderful area for classic railroading photography. Multiple tracks, frequent trains, and interesting buildings with several good vantage points make for great train watching. The area is located just west of downtown at the confluence of the Missouri and Kansas rivers.

◄ ◄ **Norfolk Southern Railway and BNSF at Sloss**—In Birmingham, several historic viaducts, some as old as the 1890s, cross the very busy main lines through the center of the city. A little further to the east stands the massive Sloss Furnaces, dating to the 1880s, and now a National Historic Landmark. As with West Bottoms in Kansas City and a number of similar settings across the country, Birmingham's viaducts are an ideal location for train watching and photography.

⋀ **(Left) San Luis & Rio Grande Railroad No. 1100**—This beautifully restored 1946 General Motors Electro-Motive Division diesel-electric locomotive can often be admired at the station in Alamosa, Colorado. The FP10 was originally built as an F3A and was rebuilt to current specifications in 2006. It is powered by a V-16 diesel rated at 1,750 horsepower and 1,300 kilowatts. The locomotive is painted in Rio Grande's dramatic, original FT color scheme. **(Right) San Luis & Rio Grande Railroad No. 115**—Painted to match No. 1100, this immaculate locomotive is an Electro-Motive Division SD90MAC43. With the "MAC" designation, it is rated at 4,300 horsepower and is an AC traction design. It was built in 1999 and rebuilt in 2009. The SD90s are no longer sold domestically due to EPA emission regulations.

INDEX

Page numbers in italics indicate an item that appears in a photograph or caption.

ABOUT THE AUTHOR

Ken Boyd holds a B.S. degree in chemistry and an MBA, and has spent his career working in the electric utility industry. He has been an avid photographer since the mid-1970s and a train and railroading enthusiast all his life. Ken has taught photography courses part-time at the University of Alabama at Birmingham and Samford University since 1985 on subjects such as darkroom techniques, creative digital compositions, and photographic processes of the 1800s. He has traveled extensively to study and photograph locomotives and other historic subjects, including watermills and antique vehicles. His photographic techniques and images have been published in numerous periodicals, books, and online sites, and he speaks regularly on photographic and locomotive topics. Beginning with the new millennia, he embraced and participated fully in the transformation of photographic imaging from film and the wet darkroom to digital capture and the computer. His approach to photography has evolved over the last four decades and today is totally unique for presenting subjects like the locomotive in a very exciting and fresh manner. He and his wife, Dj, live in Birmingham, Alabama, where most of the current Class 1 and several shortline railroads have a presence.